FROM LAYOFF TO LIFTOFF

Complimentary Promotional Edition

PRE-FINAL EDIT FORM
NOT FOR RESALE

Roger Mallory
with
Janet Helin

FROM LAYOFF TO LIFTOFF

The Beginner's Guide to Freedom and Prosperity that Anyone Can Follow

by Roger Mallory

Published by:
AnBeyond Publishing
PMB 1227
22833 Bothell Everett Highway #102
Bothell, WA 98021

Orders@AnBeyond.com
http://www.AnBeyond.com

All quotations have been attributed to the original person in so far as the author was able to find the original person quoted. If a reader discovers that our attributation is in error, we would appreciate receiving the correction for future editions.

ISBN, print ed. 1 ed 0-9744014-4-7
ISBN, PDF ed. 1 ed 0-9744014-8-X
ISBN, Audio ed. 1 ed 0-9744014-9-8

Mallory, Roger
FROM LAYOFF TO LIFTOFF: The Beginner's Guide to Freedom and Prosperity that Anyone Can Follow
P.cm.
Includes bibliographical references (p.) and index.
ISBN: 0-9744014-8-X
1. Success in Business. I. Title
2. Wealth
3. Business
4. Financial, Personal

TABLE OF CONTENTS

My Deepest Gratitude

This book is dedicated first and foremost to my wife, Marita, for it was only through her undying belief in me that this book ever came to be completed. And to my parents, Barbara and Cliff. A particular thanks to my father who is an excellent proofreader.

There are several others who had their part. Dian, thanks for the mentorship and encouragement and the foreword! Roy, Pete and Jamie, my friends who keep me in line big time! Bob and Mary, their friendship has given Marita and me so much!

The rest of my family, anchors when the sea gets rough, every one of them. Dawn, Pat, Kyle and Anna, Gordon, Sandy, Kristen and Stephanie.

And lastly, as a Christain, to my Lord Jesus, may this book be a help to all who read it.

FOREWORD

There are so many books out there about making money and owning your own business. Even more if you include books on investing. Many of these books are great resources, but there have been few books written for people who have been laid off or are facing other "job trauma."

Roger Mallory is an expert in dealing with layoffs and has been a catalyst for a number of people to venture out and create their own future by becoming investors and business owners. His unique knowledge of the needs and concerns of people going through "job trauma" allows him to help where few others can.

This book is unique in another way as well. It is based on a real life scenario where Roger and his wife, Marita took six weeks out of their lives to simulate a layoff. The content of the book is "field tested" by them. As you read the book, you will get a chance to check out excerpts of their journals during that time to see how they did. I think you will be encouraged and energized by what you find in what they did.

One last thing before I let you loose to read this book. I have only known Roger a short time, but I have come to know him as a wonderful person full of great ideas. His passion is to help others create income opportunities which empower their dreams. In the pages that follow, I think you will find some great ideas. So enjoy and happy creating!

Dian Thomas
TV Personality/Author/Professional Speaker
www.milliondollarpr.com
www.dianthomas.com

Note to Our Readers

The advice contained in this material might not be suitable for everyone. The author designed this information to present his opinion and experience about the subject matter. The reader must investigate all aspects of every business decision before committing him/herself to any course of action.

The author obtained the information presented in this book from what he considers reliable and reputable resources as well as from personal experience, but he does not imply or guarantee the veracity of the information included herein.

The author does not give legal, accounting or other advice that is the purview of licensed professionals. The author disclaims any liability, loss or risk taken by individuals who directly or indirectly act on the information contained in this book. The author believes the information provided is sound but will not take responsibility for the actions of readers or the results of those actions.

Life is not easy for any of us. But what of that? We must have perseverance and, above all, confidence in ourselves. We must believe that we are gifted for something, and that this something, at whatever cost, must be attained.
– Marie Curie

IN SEARCH OF THE ADVENTURE OF A LIFETIME

You can turn your situation into the opportunity of your life!

Stop telling God how big your mountain is and start telling your mountain how big God is. – Anonymous

Where are all the jobs in America going?

What would happen if you lost your job tomorrow? Would your world end? Could you find a new job quickly?

Would you want a new job?

Our economy is changing. In the process, it is changing everyone's lives. As the American business world migrates from its industrial base, corporate structures shift and massive layoffs result. Because of these shifts, jobs are hard to find. You can no longer count on the security of a steady corporate paycheck or career advancement. Gone are the days when you could keep one job your entire life and retire to enjoy the peaceful bliss of your golden years. You can't even depend on Social Security, if you believe what you are told by the media.

Despite the upheaval and uncertainty, people continue to make and spend money. How? By looking for and embracing new opportunities.

What if you could achieve financial independence with nothing but some planning and a great sense of adventure? Would you try it? You don't need specialized training or ideal circumstances. You need only the desire and willingness to take action to control your future.

If you have that desire, your Adventure awaits!

Why did we create the Six Week Adventure?

My wife Marita and I are an average American couple. We created the Six Week Adventure based on our typical American circumstances. The company I work for is facing unprecedented levels of change and massive layoffs. If I am laid off this time, it will be my fifth layoff during my 23-year professional career. That is pressure enough, but there's more.

After 26 years of teaching children in our public schools, Marita recently lost her teaching position. Our circumstances made us wonder what our future would hold. The only thing that remained certain was the absolute uncertainty of relying on a "steady" job! We realized things could spin out of control very quickly. The power to stop this whirlwind wasn't in our hands.

Or was it?

When Marita's mother died during the spring of 2002, we received an inheritance. The unexpected income alleviated some of our short-term financial concerns, but we knew the money wouldn't last forever. What if I lost my job just as the money ran out? What if Marita couldn't find another teaching position? We didn't want to allow this gift to dissolve into nothing. It was our wish to use the money to secure our future and honor the memory of Marita's mother. We saw an opportunity to work responsibly with our assets but we needed a plan.

Could we avoid the pitfalls others face when they deal with the loss – or threat of loss – of their jobs? Job loss or uncertainty can devastate a person's ego. A common response is to hide from the reality of the situation. We knew that whatever we did, we needed to take into account the emotional elements of financial uncertainty. We understood that our plan needed to address the high level of stress involved.

We didn't know where to start. Marita had done a magnificent job building her retirement funds, but neither of us was particularly knowledgeable about the more complex and creative investment opportunities available. We were concerned that if we tried to grow our money, we would risk huge losses on bad investments. But we were determined to find a way to make it work.

We started to read books by financial gurus such as Suze Orman, Warren Buffet, Robert Kiyosaki, Robert Allen and many others. Their advice seemed directed toward ordinary people who didn't have specialized financial knowledge. People like us. As we turned from one page to the next, our path became apparent. After we finished Allen's *Multiple Streams of Income,* we realized our financial security depended on an action plan to set up sources of income for ourselves. We decided to give it a try.

We took a page from Allen's experience and gave ourselves a challenge. We decided to allow ourselves six weeks to set things in motion.

It felt like a dress rehearsal for

February 16, 2003
Roger's journal entry

Wow! We have only one week left until Marita and I start on our way to our adventure. A number of things are in motion and we are excited and getting antsy to head to Florida!

Because this is my inaugural entry for this online journal, I want to bullet list some of what has happened to this point.

In May 2002, we lost my mother-in-law rather quickly and unexpectedly. It was very hard on both Marita and I. Her mother left us an inheritance, so we started to read every investment book we could find. I devoured everything from Napoleon Hill to Robert Kiyosaki. I was determined not to squander a penny of what this wonderful lady had left us! It was at this point that I found the *Multiple Streams of Income* book by Robert G. Allen

In September 2002, we started a concerted effort to get in line with the first four chapters of the *Multiple Streams of Income* Book. After

what we would do if I were laid off. A dry run, if you will, to prepare for the day we had to make our living without the security of the aerospace industry. We knew that at the end of the six weeks we wouldn't be millionaires. But we'd have a framework in place... a framework we hoped would lead to our first million by the end of the year. We continued to read and research opportunities. We read book after book on everything from Stock investing to marketing. We learned so much and yet had so much more to learn. Because of our reading and our burning desire to succeed, a plan started to emerge. As we formulated our plan, we spent a great deal of time trying to determine which types of income streams would be most suitable for us. We thought long and hard and we prayed just as long and hard. After much soul searching and good old-fashioned research, we decided to set aside six weeks to put new income systems into place.

six months of doing what Allen suggested in the first four chapters, I can tell you that I see a six-figure difference!

In November 2002, I signed up for one of Allen's challenges.

Wow, what a bunch of stuff to learn! To start out, I was focused on Real Estate and Marita wanted to concentrate on Stocks. As we started to listen to Allen's teleconferences, I started to focus in on the Internet, infopreneur and marketing calls as more of a curiosity than anything else. Resulting from those calls, I have pursued as my second course of study infopreneuring with an Internet flavor.

Well, that got us to the New Year. My next installment will bring you up to the present.

For our Six Week Adventure from February to April 2003, we set two major goals. First was to increase our net assets to a point beyond one million dollars. Secondly we wanted to set up sources of income that would sustain themselves and grow. With a focus on two major streams – Real Estate and Stock Market investments – and one small Network Marketing stream, we launched specific projects intended to generate short- and long-term income.

We knew the systems we set up would allow us to protect our inheritance, act responsibly with our assets and grow our money into a million within a reasonable period of time. We hoped that within the year, these sources of income would allow us the freedom not to worry about corporate restructuring, downsizing or job loss.

Ours is a plan created by ordinary people for ordinary people under what have become sadly ordinary conditions: a sluggish economy, massive layoffs, shifts in corporate cultures and international unrest. Ours is a plan anyone can follow. We followed it. You can too!

From Our Newsletter

This is the first issue of our weekly newsletter. Marita and I are so excited to have you join us in this adventure of ours! As I compose this newsletter, we are looking at a mere five days before the official start of what I have fondly called among my friends "our little experiment." But, the truth is that it is not so little! We are doing nothing short of remarkable! We are going to change our lives completely in only six weeks!

For me, the coolest part is that we are going to do it in such a way as to make friends and help others catch the vision of changing their lives. We are giving away books at sixweekadventure.com. We are talking to a whole lot of wonderful, talented people. We are also learning from the ideas and talents of our advisors. And we are going to have a number of other surprises for you in the coming weeks.

Already, we have given away three Nothing Down books to our very first subscribers! I have some ideas for the 100th subscriber and the 500th and beyond! If you sponsor a winner (just email me with their address at submit@anbeyond.com), you will get the same reward!

Another thing I want to do is share a few business ideas in this newsletter on a weekly basis. I am coming across so many good ideas that my wife and I can't even hope to try all of them! "So, " I said to myself, "why don't you share them on this newsletter!" You just might be able to put some of them into action."

We are firming up a number of other ideas for the six weeks. I have some interesting possibilities for my Real Estate business and Marita is going to be starting the Stock investing in a couple of weeks as well! We have purchased some Tax Lien certificates in Arizona in a partnership we have established down there. These are really exciting.

PART I

CREATE YOUR ADVENTURE
A new hope: Getting on with your future

The problem is not being laid off, it is not seeing the opportunity that being laid off presents!
– Roger Mallory

CHAPTER 1
WHY YOU CAN DO WHAT WE DID!

It is in the compelling zest of high adventure and of victory, and in creative action, that man finds his supreme joys.
– Antoine de Saint-Exupery

Consider the world you work in currently

Before you ask yourself whether or not you can do what we did, ask yourself why you *should* do it. We no longer live in a world where you work for the same company for 40 years and then retire quietly to a warmer climate. The average employee stays with a job as little as two to three years then moves on, either by choice or necessity. Jobs continue to move offshore. Companies continue to streamline as they attempt to become more flexible, to meet their own economic challenges. The day of the steady paycheck and solid career track is no more.

But that doesn't mean you can't maintain and significantly increase your income. You can find literally thousands of ways to earn income from multiple sources. The key is to start looking away from the corporate paycheck and in the direction of investments and entrepreneurial efforts. We chose Real Estate and the Stock Market as our principle sources of income, but you will find many others to choose from. Later in this book, we will discuss many of them. For now, it's enough that you realize how many opportunities await you.

We live in a unique time. The economy is down but won't stay that way forever. If you can find new sources of income during a down economy, imagine what you'll encounter on the upside! The businesses and opportunities are genuinely there if you are willing to act on them.

Now is your time. The 21st century has ushered in a new and vibrant small-business economy. Possibilities abound as this new economic movement gains momentum... possibilities for people like you and me. If your job is in jeopardy, if you are weary of the daily, thankless grind or if your company is going through a series of layoffs, you can change your future for the better. The opportunity is great and it is at your feet if you choose to take it!

Aside from ending your worries about job security, why else should you take on the Six Week Adventure? With financial independence comes freedom. Not only will you be free of your concerns about employment, but you'll also be free to work on your own terms. You can work when, where and how you want. You can give your family the quality time they deserve. Pay more attention to your health. Have time and disposable income for charitable causes that perpetuate your values.

Carpe diem: Seize your day... or six weeks

Now that you've agreed you *should* take the Six Week Adventure, we'll tell you why you can do it. Marita and I are real people who lead hectic lives in the everyday world of 21st century America. We didn't start our Adventure with any specialized financial expertise. Check out our journals at **http://www.anbeyond.com/sixweeks/dailyreport/index.htm** and you'll see exactly where we started! But we succeeded and are still prospering. You can too.

To set up multiple sources of income requires desire, confidence, thoughtful planning and networking. You'll find opportunities where you might not have looked before. You'll receive support from places where you least expect it. The Six Week Adventure system works because you approach opportunities differently than you might have in the past. You look carefully and deliberately for ways to set up income streams. You don't react. You *act*.

The Six Week Adventure system and this book were created to help you take action. This is not just another book about life change, career change or investing. *It is a guide to help you take active control of your finances.* Most Americans don't. They are content to bounce around at the whim of others: boss, family, government or someone else. Our system will help *you* be the one to call the shots concerning your personal finances and freedom.

After you take inventory of your resources, abilities and needs, you'll set systems in place that will generate new sources of income for you. For six weeks or longer, you will concentrate on setting up those systems and getting income streams started. Then you'll focus on maintaining your new sources of income. You'll be surprised how quickly you will

February 19, 2003
Marita's journal entry

I have tried to journal before. I start out with the best of intentions, continue for a few days then drop out. Life and the world interrupt and somehow I can't find the time to write. Then there is the problem of content: what can I possibly write about?

Now today, I prepare with my husband, Roger, as we begin a six-week experience on looking into our wants, needs, dreams and financial situation, and how to improve in these areas. As part of this process, I promised to write down my side of the six-week adventure.

My dream is not to return to a teaching position in the school system. To do this I need to be financially sound. I have been fortunate to have a year off to review what I want for Roger and me. I want to be a stay at home wife and mother of an adopted child. We have been in the process of adoption for a good year. But it takes money to cover my missing income.

In planning for the future, I had great role models in my parents. My father, a self-employed halibut fisherman had to plan how to use the money he earned to support his family from season to season, cover the

start to approach the million-dollar level.

We chose a six-week time frame for our Adventure. Certainly you can take more time and possibly less. However, we recommend six weeks be the minimum amount of time you devote to setting your Adventure in motion. The six weeks will allow you to go through an entire month and experience one full monthly financial "cycle."

One other reason I chose six weeks was that it was approximately the same length as my previous job hunts that followed my layoffs. Once I got over the shock of the layoff, I have always been able to find work in less than six weeks. Thus, six weeks seemed a reasonable amount of time that represented a minimal risk in the larger scheme of things.

We will discuss later in this book the ways you can evaluate your situation to determine the period of time you can allow for your Adventure. It wouldn't hurt at this point to start thinking about your current obligations and the timeframe you might have available.

You are the only person who can decide if you are ready to take financial control of your life. If you are, this book will tell you where and how to start. We'll go over the concrete steps you need to take.

cost of college for his two children and plan retirement for both himself and my mom. He achieved this through savings and investments.

From the time I got my first bank account at six months of age, I started to save. This included the weekly school banking days, putting money in other saving accounts, and pairing with my Dad to get the best interest rates on money market funds. When I was in high school, my parents met with a financial planner and invested in mutual funds. The investor's motto was "invest in yourself first." So began my first mutual fund.

Gradually, through prodding from friends and family, I planned for my retirement. I bought a condo, invested in Tax Shelter Annuities, IRAs, income funds, money market funds and savings.

Then I met Roger in 1999. I began to dream new dreams with him. My retirement goals and needs changed. I came into this marriage with only my condo and car payments. Roger had student loans, not much in savings, but he had turned things around and was taking good care of his finances. The past two years in marriage has been a time to view our saving and spending habits. Now it is time to

Here is a little Acronym that I would like to give you. Remember the word ACT:

***A** ccept that you can do it.*

***C** reate your future, don't let others do it for you.*

***T** ake action now!*

If you are ready to act, read on. It's time to seize the day... and your six weeks!

February 23, 2003
Marita's journal entry

Today, I'm seated at a table outdoors in the Florida sunshine. Roger is working on his stuff back inside the room we call home for a few days. I needed to get out and get some sunshine and Vitamin D. I'm out by the volleyball court, full of inviting sand, next to the pool among the palm trees and the southern pines. No one is out here. I hear voices and music coming from one of the units and a plane flying over an otherwise peaceful, solitary environment.

It is hard to believe it is February. This feels like summer back in Seattle. It would be a perfect Sunday to drive out to my cabin. My cabin is co-owned by my brother and his family, myself and Roger. I mention this because it is one of the reasons I'm interested in changing our life and the flow of money and finances.

Today, officially, begins our Six Week Adventure. We are in Orlando, four days before the start of the Enlightened Millionaire Retreat. I'm filled with a mixture of fear and excitement. My stomach aches from fear, I think. My mind is filled with excitement, adventure and hope. My heart flutters with a mixture of both, because of the unknown, the risk and the anticipation that we are going to "do" instead of just talk.

I have many questions. The basic one is "How?" And yet I know how: Real Estate, Internet, and Stocks. But how do we get started? I'm doing Stocks. I need the time to watch, the time to paper trade, and the time to get information. One thing that I have is some cash to do it.

Part of our trip to Orlando – and the reason we arrived here a few days before the seminars actually begin – is for relaxation. To have some fun, soak up some of the sun's rays and spend time talking with Roger to make plans for what our days in this six-week adventure should deal with. I also want my responsibilities defined. What I want to do is be the supporter, the helper. Roger has the ideas. I also want to become more visionary, coming up with ideas that I have passion about. I feel blocked. My hope is for this seminar is to help me focus on those ideas, find the passion, develop vision, and then act. I need to bring this to the Lord in prayer. So a part of our days need to be spent in communication and celebration with our God.
I'll go make footprints in the sand as I set back to our room and check on Roger. Let the adventure begin.

A wise man will make more opportunities than he finds.
- Sir Francis Bacon

CHAPTER 2
YOUR DECISIONS MATTER

What lies behind us and what lies before us are small matters compared to what lies within us.

– Ralph Waldo Emerson

Decide to do something now!

Now that you realize you can take control of your situation, you will understand why every decision you make is important. Are you ready and willing to look at your situation differently, to move toward a new type of financial security and freedom? Your shift in focus comes as a result of some important decisions. The first decision you must make right now is this: Decide to take action, to do something immediately to set your future in motion.

Don't think that because you are going through difficulties you have to be paralyzed. We designed the Six Week Adventure for people who live in the real world of the 21st century. This includes people who face difficult situations in terms of employment or financial security. This book offers a concrete idea that can help you move forward regardless of your circumstances. You can take charge right now and make significant strides toward eliminating your financial uncertainty.

When faced with job loss or other financial insecurity, most people enter a cycle of grief. Though not always in this order, most people go through each of five phases:[1]

- **Denial:** the loss did not happen
- **Anger:** the loss should not have happened
- **Bargaining:** how can we prevent the loss?
- **Depression:** the full impact of the loss overwhelms us
- **Acceptance:** we accept the loss and resume our lives

Even when a person tries not to fall into this cycle, these emotions creep in unexpectedly. If you are not prepared for them, they can make it very difficult for you to move on. Opportunities will pass by because you are still looking backward, unable to let go of the way things were.

Fear is a byproduct of the first four stages of grief. Fear can paralyze you. You have a choice to make. Give in to the fear – or pretend the grief won't affect you – and do nothing to control the situation. As a result, the situation will get worse. Or you can acknowledge that the grief is real and allow yourself the freedom to

February 24, 2003
Roger's journal entry

As we launch into this adventure ours, I am struck by the breadth of what we are trying to do. Yes, we are trying to get over the million-dollar mark, but there is a lot more here. We are trying to change the way we think, the way we deal with our health and how we act on ideas and dreams.

One of the most amazing things that has happened to us – especially me – is that my thinking has changed. For so long, I have been what my good friend Jamie calls a wage slave. You know the drill: go to work, do the work, come home, eat, watch TV and go to bed only to get up again the next morning to repeat the process. A decent living can be made that way, but it is not as secure as some might think. I have been laid off three times since 1988.

The last three months have seen a change in the way I think about making a living. I am using my imagination more and I am very excited about the possibilities

grieve. If you address your grief constructively, you can move through it, put everything behind you and move on with the next phase of your life... a better phase!

What more constructive way to deal with your difficult circumstances than to view them as the key to your future? Without the job loss or financial uncertainty you face, you might have been content to continue to limit your possibilities. *That* would have been cause for grief! Now you have the perfect reason to get started on a new future: a future with unlimited possibilities.

Dr. Karl Menninger, author of ***Whatever Became of Sin*** commented that when you become depressed, you should get up and get out of your house, lock the door behind you, go across the tracks and help somebody. The message here for those who have lost their jobs or face possible layoffs is to get out and do something constructive, to take control of the situation. Job loss is what you make of it. If you want it to be the end, it will be the end. If you consider job loss to represent an opportunity for a new beginning, your future will look increasingly bright.

Corporate restructuring and downsizing is beyond your control. Loss of your job as a result of economic shifts is not your fault. You can't go back and change things, and the outcome wouldn't be different even if you could. Instead of worrying about a situation you did not control, get ready to create a set of circumstances you *can* control. Get ready to build your financial future

for the future. I think this holds true for Marita as well. We are now thinking about how we can do things rather than how they can't be done. The impossible is becoming possible in our lives.

Part of the challenge to me is to become more responsible with my health. Marita has agreed to do this with me. We have decided to get up every morning and walk. We are also going to change our diet. Actually, we are continuing an effort we started last September. At this point, we are going to make some habit changes. I am healthier than I have been in years. Now it is time to take the next steps.

It is a lot, but any change has many facets. We are going to be very focused during this time, not just exclusively on money.

based on decisions only *you* make and actions *you* take.

It is important to keep things in perspective. For every difficulty that threatens to keep a person from succeeding, thousands of other people have had it worse and succeeded despite the obstacles. You can too.

Know where you stand

"Confidence is a habit that can be developed by acting as if you already had the confidence you desire to have." These words of Brian Tracy[2] are great advice, if you are willing to examine your current situation so you know exactly where you stand. Let's talk a little about how to gain that confidence and act as if you already have it.

Your success depends on how honest you are with yourself. You must start by taking full account of your current situation, including what you want to change and how you plan to make those changes. To move forward, you need to determine your goals. You must also devise a concrete plan that will move you toward those goals. You need a roadmap.

The key to creating a roadmap is knowledge. You can achieve your goals, however grand, as long as you know where you're going. You can determine where you are going only if you know where you are right now. Take some time to assess your situation. Figure out where you are, and then you will know where to go next and how to get there. Then get ready to take your first step.

You desire to fundamentally change your life, don't you?

"Your self-confidence is directly connected to how much you feel you are making a difference in your world." Again, the words of Brian Tracy highlight an important aspect of the Six Week Adventure. You have the power to change things, to make a difference in the world – and in your life.

One of the best lessons taught by the reality of cor-

From The Newsletter

I want to share with you three things I think are essential to any entrepreneurial venture: means, audacity and courage. I have them listed here in order of importance, starting with the least important.

To be an entrepreneur you must have some means to move forward on a project. This is so obvious that I am sure some of you are giving me a big "DUH!" But it is the obvious stuff that will either stop or prevent you from starting. It is this very thing idea that has kept me from my visions. The reason I use the word means rather than money is key to what I am trying to communicate. In today's world of information, you don't need money as your only means. You have ideas, energy and imagination, all of which have value in the right market. All you need is the audacity to go out and find your market.

The Merriam-Webster dictionary defines audacity as: a: intrepid boldness and b: bold or arrogant disregard of normal restraints. The whole concept of going forward and starting your own business or selling an idea demands the ability to step out and get noticed. To be audacious – in this context – means to break through constraints that hold you back in order to pursue your ideas. It is uncomfortable, I know. Right now my wife and I are putting ourselves in front of you in our SIx Week Adventure. We are experiencing our share of anxiety these days. But it is important that we keep our audacity. You will also find many people out there who will support you and give you the courage you need to be audacious! We certainly have received a great deal of support.

Courage is the one ingredient in the formula that allows you to be audacious, which gives you the ability to listen to your dreams more. It is not recklessness; it does not embolden you to do dangerous things. However, it is this quality that will allow you to be bold and take the risks necessary to break through to the success you crave. This is the quality I admire most in the successful people I know. It is the lynchpin to success.

These three things: means, audacity and courage have revolutionized our lives. I hope you find something here that can help you.

Here is a quick business idea for an easy start in practicing these three principles. Find a Network Marketing product and find different ways to market it.

Try the internet. Go to fairs, shows and festivals and ply your wares there. Try conventional retail avenues. Try doing the party route. In short, use your imagination and do your business!

porate restructuring is the lesson most often missed. The threat of job loss looms greater with each passing year. Uncertainty grows, and with it, questions about financial security. In response, most people look for solutions within the same system that caused this turmoil. They look for another corporate job, either before or after they lose theirs. They search for security within the same structure that caused their insecurity.

You have the power to break free of this cycle. If your future seems uncertain, if you don't call *all* the shots that affect your well being, if you question whether your actions make a difference, consider this as a sign things need to change. Don't escape job loss by looking for another job. Take control and move forward on your own terms.

Any major life change must be your decision. Dare to do great things and you might fail. You also might gain – more than you imagined. Dare to do nothing, however, and you will gain nothing.

The resolve to do the Adventure is within you

Dale Carnegie said, "Take a chance! All life is a chance. The man who goes the furthest is generally the one who is willing to do and dare. The sure thing boat never gets far from shore." It is my belief that each of you can lift yourself up and do the things you dream about. You have the ability and the fortitude to do the things in life that are calling you, if only you allow yourself to believe you can do it. It is that simple. Henry Ford said, "Whether you think you can or you think you can't, you are probably right!"

What holds us back? For me and for most of you, it is having too selective and too long of a memory. Most people remember the bad things much more easily than the good. I've heard it takes at least four good memories to balance a bad one. I believe this. I have lived a pretty great life and yet I often sulk over the bad things I have gone through.

The human mind has such an amazing ability to recall the past. This is good if we use our memories to help us repeat the good things in our past and avoid repeating our mistakes. But memory can also hold us back. If you combine the human penchant for remembering the bad stuff with our natural ability to remember things from long ago, it's easy to become very disappointed and convinced we cannot do anything. Don't believe it!

Let's depart from the reading here and do a little exercise. This will take 30 minutes to an hour. Take the following instructions with a pad of paper and a pen or pencil to a table with a telephone. Here's what I want you to do:

1. On the pad of paper, write down ten great and wonderful memories. Leave a few lines after each item.

2. Now under each of those memories, write down some of the people who played a role in creating those memories.

3. You probably have the phone numbers of two or three of those people. Call them and tell them you were thinking about that good time. Enjoy a little conversation.

Now that your conversations are over, you feel better about things, don't you? Allow yourself to be the sum of the good that has been in your life! Enjoy your accomplishments and revel in the friendships you have gained

****

A pessimist sees the difficulty in every opportunity;
an optimist sees the opportunity in every difficulty.
- Sir Winston Churchill

over the years. Learn to live on the positive side of your life.

Take a look at the following list that highlights turning points in the life of Abraham Lincoln:

YEAR	**FAILURES and/or SETBACKS**
1832	Lost job and was defeated for state legislature
1833	Failed in business
1835	Sweetheart died
1836	Had nervous breakdown
1838	Defeated for Speaker
1843	Defeated for nomination for Congress
1848	Lost re-nomination
1849	Rejected for land officer
1854	Defeated for U.S. Senate
1856	Defeated in nomination for Vice President
1858	Again defeated for U.S. Senate
AND FINALLY	
1860	Elected President

Quite a list, and it doesn't even include the loss of two of his four children before his death. What was Lincoln's secret? I believe Lincoln was able to reach the presidency because he was resilient and focused. Resilient in that he came back better and stronger after each failure. Focused in that he was able to put the past behind him and concentrate on the tasks at hand in order to create his future. He did not look back. He took courage and went forward to become the president considered to be our greatest ever!

Can you do the Adventure we talk about in this book? It is designed to help you put the past into perspective and focus on your future. Can you learn to focus and take a constructive view of your past? I believe you can. But you have to believe it too!

Every person I have ever met has the capacity to succeed and learn how to focus. May I humbly ask you to Consider that you can too? Your Adventure awaits!

Can you allow yourself to be creative?

Creativity is a catalyst of change. Unless you create a new path for yourself and find a new way to approach your financial security, you will not scc your way clear of the work cycle you are in now. Opportunities for change exist, but you must think creatively to make these opportunities work for you.

Creativity is at the center of almost all success. This book is about creating a new way of doing things. We don't want to create your future for you. Instead we offer you the knowledge tools and support to create it yourself.

To set up new sources of income, you will need to imagine a different way of doing things. You will need to recognize possibilities and maximize opportunities. The more creative you are prepared to be, the more opportunities you will find, and the harder you will work to make them successful.

In his groundbreaking work ***Think and Grow Rich***, Napoleon Hill writes that imagination is a characteristic of successful millionaires. So let's do a little imagining with the following scenario.

****

It is not because things are difficult
that we do not dare;
it is because we do not dare
that they are difficult.
- Seneca,

Let's say you need $60, 000 a year to live independently and that you have some cash stowed away. And let's say you love woodworking. You can accomplish your goal using a multiple sources approach:

Stream	**Earned**
Buy an "ugly" house, fix it and sell it for an average profit of $15, 000. Buy and sell two houses per year (or four at $7, 500).	30, 000
Learn a good short-term strategy in the Stock Market and get a 10% return on your $50, 000 investment.	$5, 000
Write a book, self-publish and sell 5, 000 copies in the first year at a clear profit of $2 per book after all costs are figured.	$10, 000
Create a line of crafts that you sell at art shows and in local shops.	$5, 000
Take a part-time job at the local woodworking store and teach classes there as well. You will receive an hourly wage in addition to the fees you receive for teaching the class.	$10, 000

If $60, 000 isn't enough for you to live on, how about getting $100, 000 a year from the same plan expanded a little bit?

Stream	**Earned**
Buy an "ugly" house, fix it and sell it for an average profit of $15, 000. Buy and sell four houses per year (or six at $10, 000).	$60, 000

Stream	Earned
Learn a good short-term strategy in the Stock Market and get a 10% return on your $70, 000 investment.	$7, 000
Write a book, self-publish and sell 5, 000 copies in the first year at a clear profit of $2 per book after all costs are figured.	$10, 000
Create a line of crafts that you sell at art shows and in local shops. Develop a wholesale business to go along with your retail enterprise.	$10, 000
Take a part-time job at the local woodworking store and teach classes there as well. You will receive an hourly wage in addition to the fees you receive for teaching the class. Also offer one-on-one onsite training.	$10, 000

You can build a plan like this, one or a few blocks at a time. All you need is to consider different sources of income, to move beyond the bounds shaped by the mentality that accompanies a corporate paycheck. The Six Week Adventure will help focus your imagination, creativity and will-power so you can achieve your own long-term plan.

"Things may come to those who wait, " Abraham Lincoln said. "But only the things left by those who hustle." Opportunities are out there waiting for you. This book teaches you how to look farther and deeper, to recognize and seize one opportunity after another.

Does the Six Week Adventure sound too good to be true? Remember that things are only too good to be true when you don't act on them.

THE TEN COMPONENTS OF RESILIENCY[3]

Unambivalent Commitment to Life.
The common core of resilient people is this transcendent attitude or belief which gives them the passion and courage to bounce back.

Self-confidence.
Resilient people believe they can understand the world around them, set realistic goals to achieve, and develop the skills required to do so.

Adaptability.
Resilient people can modify their habits to work with others, personally and professionally.

Resourcefulness.
Resilient people know what resources are available for problem-solving and where they can turn for support.

Willingness to Risk.
The resilient person doesn't always play it "safe" but takes intelligent risk grounded in real possibilities and with a good chance for success.

Accept Personal Responsibility.
Resilient people have a strong philosophical or spiritual belief in self-determination. They do not claim to be victims or make excuses for mistakes. By owning their mistakes, they turn them into positive learning experiences.

Perspective.
Resilient people know what is important and what is not. They put their energy into serious or core issues and activities and business – or enjoy – the inconsequential ones.

Openness to new ideas.
Resilient people taking new information eagerly without excessive prejudgment or critical analysis.

Willingness to be proactive.
Resilient people meet challenge with positive action rather than reaction.

Attentiveness.
Resilient people are paying attention to the world around them. When others speak, they are listening.

PART II

SET YOUR FOUNDATION
Your Four Keys to a Successful Adventure

All of us have schnozzles... if not in our face then in our character, minds or habits. When we admit our schnozzles instead of defending them, we begin to laugh and the world laughs with us.
– Jimmy Durante

CHAPTER 3
KEY 1: CREATE YOUR LIFE INVENTORY

People, when they first come to America, whether as travelers or settlers, become aware of a new and agreeable feeling: that the whole country is their oyster.
– Alistair Cooke

Now that you are ready to change your situation, to take control of your life, you need to do a little preparation. We know you can do it. In the next four chapters we share our experience and advice to help you begin your Adventure.

Review your current situation

Remember that to reach your goals you must know your starting point. Start with an honest and comprehensive assessment of your situation. You will need to look at your financial situation as well as intangibles such as your emotional readiness to take on this life-altering challenge. An initial inventory gives you not only a clear understanding of what resources you have available to facilitate your journey. It also gives you a realistic perspective. You'll know exactly where you are going and what it will take to get there.

You can take inventory using any method that helps you see the big picture. You do not need knowledge of accounting techniques to do this, though you might consider talking to a financial advisor. You simply need a way to determine what resources you have available so that you begin this journey on a realistic footing. We will share with you what we did.

We created a balance sheet to determine exactly where we were financially at the start of our Adventure. We used a yellow pad, but in retrospect we should have used a spreadsheet. Eventually we did create a spreadsheet that you can find on our website:

http://www.anbeyond.com/lotlo/SAS.xls.

Our balance sheet included four separate columns:

- Assets – savings, real property, bonds, etc.
- Debts – mortgage, bills, etc.
- Income – wages, investment income, etc.
- Liquid Assets

We took a financial inventory and listed all items under the appropriate column. You may download our spreadsheet as a model but you don't have to follow it exactly. Feel free to do this any way you'd like, but try to get the following important totals:

- Total Assets
- Total Labilities
- Total Assets - Total Liabilities
- Total Monthly Income
- Total Monthly Outlay
- Total Monthly Income - Total Monthly Outlay

After we added/subtracted all four totals, we were surprised to learn where we stood financially. No doubt you will be surprised at what you learn from your own assessment. After you complete your financial inventory, ask yourself:

- Are your finances positive or negative?
- What would be the effect of an absence of income for the duration of your Adventure?
- Do you have assets you can use to kick-start your Adventure?
- Do you have excessive debt? If so, how do you plan to reduce it?
- Can some of your assets be leveraged or converted... and should they?

This exercise should generate additional questions unique to your situation. While these are difficult questions to consider, they are absolutely vital. The Six Week Adventure is an experience that will alter your financial situation, and before you begin you need to know exactly what you are willing – and not willing – to do in order to change your circumstances. You need to answer these questions honestly before you develop a six-week plan.

For our Adventure, we had the benefit of our inheritance to work with. I was able to take six weeks off from work to concentrate on setting new income streams into place. Marita was already without her job. We could have taken out a second mortgage on our house, which had appreciated significantly. We did not need to do this. It is not advisable to over-leverage assets. I would only consider using your home's equity if you are very confident in your plan and have no other assets. Regardless, that's a decision only you can make.

If you do not have assets to invest in your Adventure, you can set up income streams that require little or no cash up front. Nothing-Down Real Estate investments and Internet income sources are great examples of streams you can set up immediately. Meanwhile you can start to save and focus on future sources of income. Learn everything you can about those streams while you save.

Each person's financial situation is different. It doesn't matter what your starting point is. The important first step is to take inventory and determine where you are financially right now.

Your emotional inventory is just as important. The purpose of these initial assessments – financial or otherwise – is to determine what resources will help you on your Adventure and what types of action you are willing to take. Following are some exercises that will help you prepare for your Adventure. Honest answers to these questions are critical to your success.

1. Write down how each member of your family views money:
   a. Is it evil?
   b. Is it important?
   c. What purpose does it serve?
   d. Does it cause stress?

Try to think of at least six more attitudes toward money and discuss them. Many people have never discussed attitudes toward money with other members of their family. Money can be a volatile source of disagreement. Family members need to be aware that attitude toward

March 4, 2003
Roger's journal entry

It is Tuesday of the second week of our Six Week Adventure and we have returned home from Orlando. We don't have any journal entries for yesterday. We spent the first half of the day at the Disney World Magic Kingdom and the rest of the day traveling home. I figured you would not want to hear my review of Pirates of the Caribbean. Nor would you want to hear my review of the legroom on American Airlines as I slept away most of the nine hours of the flight!

Today started the real meat of the effort. My first task was to drop by the mortgage broker and drop off the final papers for pre-qualification. As many of you know, most Real Estate agents won't give the time of day to you without a pre-qual. Now I know some people say I shouldn't bother with those types of agents. However, I want to have the widest and friendliest access to these people as I can. You never know when you might be working with one of them.

I did a lot of calling and setting up my systems

money is a sensitive area that concerns deeply held beliefs and mores.

2. What is your attitude about your current income streams?
   a. Are you afraid of the future?
   b. Are you frustrated?
   c. Are you happy with where you are?

Try to think of at least seven more attitudes toward your current income streams and discuss them. This discussion should be more healing than confrontational. It should allow you to feel more comfortable expressing your frustrations and concerns. When you are able to freely discuss your frustration with job prospects, investments and other sources of income, you can start thinking about your readiness to diversify income and to reach a point of reduced stress.

today. I made five calls in the morning and did some work on the website. On my way back from the broker, I took the long route and found eight interesting Real Estate prospects. When I got home, I called about another house only a few blocks from here. A beautiful place that I find fascinating and intriguing. I am expecting a call back on it soon.

All in all a great day. I believe Marita is very much on board with this as of now. I am hoping to get her journal entries caught up in the next day or two.

3. What is your personality type?
   a. Are you a risk taker or do you seek safety?
   b. Are you easily frustrated or do you push through difficulties?
   c. Are you driven by logic or feelings?
   d. Are you extroverted or introverted?
   e. Are you supportive of your spouse, if you have one?
   f. How would you characterize each of your family relationships?

Write down your answers. If you can, take a Myers-Briggs Type Indicator inventory. All adults in the family should take this inventory. It is a great tool for self-discovery. For an excellent resource for getting this test, contact me at **rm@anbeyond.com**.

Marita and I are personality opposites. I am a risk taker and Marita is a safety type. I tend to be more of a Leader/Director while Marita falls more into the amiable category. We are very supportive of each other, though, and we strive to meet in the middle where we can unite in a stronger effort.

The rest of our family on both sides has been supportive of our Adventure and has not interfered. In fact, my father and mother are very interested in what we are doing. They have consulted with us throughout our Adventure.

You'll also want to evaluate your current work situation and determine whether or not you can devote your full attention to your Adventure. If you are still employed and can't get the time away from work, you can try to take on your Adventure part time. You can scale it down and follow a slower pace. You might set up one income stream and expand when you are able.

If you work for a large corporation and can afford to take time off but don't have that much vacation time, look into taking an educational leave. Companies often pay for you to take a business or accounting class. Take the minimum number of course hours necessary to qualify for an educational leave. You'll get the time off and the class can become part of your Adventure.

If you have just gone through a layoff, now is the perfect time to start your Six Week Adventure. If you have savings or a severance package to invest in your Adventure, all the better. In many cases, investment income will not be assessed against your unemployment insurance. Check with your state unemployment office and financial advisor to be certain.

If you have lost your job and do not have extra income to invest in your Adventure, do not give up on the idea. Before you jump back into another corporate job, read the suggestions in this book and follow the preparation exercises. Consider your non-financial resources such as talent and skill – we address those in the next section.

Use that knowledge not only to position or retrain for employment but also to start a scaled-down version of the Six Week Adventure.

If you desire to change your life, our system will help you move forward. It doesn't matter where you start. What is important is that you have a clear understanding of your financial and emotional starting points.

March 4, 2003
Marita's journal entry

Life and the world got in the way of my journaling. For me, it was fun in the sun in Florida and then attending Robert Allen's seminars, which were filled with lots of information and ideas. It will take me a few days to sort it all out and apply what I learned.

I went into the seminars without a clue as to what I should expect.
I did want to come away with passion to do the job and a chance to generate some ideas for myself. I feel I have found the passion, and the desire to make a new living for us, especially after listening to the different presentations.

I also gained insight into why Roger has been so keen and eager to be self-employed. He really has an entrepreneur's heart and mind. He was jazzed about all the people he met who were just like him. He came away with lots of ideas as to how we can work together to produce a life in which we can spend more time together and have the financial backing to do so.

Getting to know your talents, skills and passion

You bring more than financial resources to your Adventure. Your talents and skills will go a long way toward your success. They are great resources. In many ways, they are your most valuable resources. Don't neglect them. Think about how you will apply them to your Adventure.

Start by taking inventory. Your talent inventory consists of two separate columns, one for talents and one for skills. Your lists will be a bit subjective, but remember, these lists are about you. One person's talent is another's hard-earned skill. The following lists will give you an example:

Talents

- Singing
- Sports
- Cooking
- Painting (Rembrandt, etc.)
- Listening

Skills

- Fly tying for fly fishing
- Woodworking
- Car repair
- Computers
- Photography

Make a comprehensive list of items under each column. Do not be modest. Your assessment of your talents and skills will help you see possibilities when you start to create your six-week plan.

Share your lists with at least three trusted people who know you well, including your spouse. Allow them to add to your list. Do not allow them to subtract from it.

After your lists are as complete as you can make them, create a new list: "Passions." Which items on your talents and skills lists are you passionate about? Not everyone gets tremendous enjoyment out of all the things they do well. Go through your lists and highlight everything at which you excel *and* find exciting. Add those items to your passions list.

I'll give you an example of why it's important to figure out which talents and skills you're passionate about. When I was in high school, I was somewhat gifted at math. Not many of my friends knew it and fewer probably cared. But here is

Well, we have returned from the ***Enlightened Millionaire Retreat*** and I must say I am feeling very enlightened! It is amazing to me that there are so many great ideas out there, and so many good people to implement them! WOW! With this in mind, I want to share a number of thoughts with you regarding what I learned.

First, a number of participants were *very* careful with the way they said things. It was wonderful to be among a group of people who consider their words, and are thoughtful about what those words really mean. Words and phrases like: "maybe, " "might, " "hope to" and "I guess so" are in our language for a reason. However, they can sabotage how a person goes about achieving his/her goals. I have a new respect for how I use language when I talk about my goals and dreams. Words like "can, " "will, " "resolve" and "know" will become more commonplace in my vocabulary!

Second, the spiritual element of success was very evident at the retreat. As an evangelical Christian, I was encouraged to see so many like-minded people.

the kicker: I hated math!

In my senior year, I took the most advanced course available to me: Math Analysis. I was a solid C student because I hated the subject. Near the end of the school year, we took a national test that rated all students on a percentile basis and I scored in the 96th percentile. My teacher, an exchange teacher from England, gave me quite the lecture when she received those scores! Why did I pull barely average grades in class when I was in the top four percent nationally? Simply put, I hated the subject!

My point? Don't do the stuff you don't like. I did pretty well with the Stock Market a few years back and even got out at the right time. But it was too much like math class. Now that Stock Market investing is a smart bet again, I have no interest in doing the work. Fortunately my wife does, so she is working the Stock Market for us.

In high school, I was advised engineering would be my best bet for a career. That's because my weakest subjects were English and the liberal arts. Nevertheless, I went to college and got a liberal arts degree in communications with an English minor. And now I am writing this book. Why? Because I love it!

Do the things you love. If you are weak in them, just work with

A large number of other faith systems were represented as well. Since the retreat was a secular event, it is nice to know that my beliefs were respected and not abused by those who have different values and had the stage. All who succeed in this world must take care of their lives spiritually. I can get so focused on something I forget to take care of my whole person. I will not allow myself to fall into that trap during this project. I want to succeed and we need all the help we can get!

Third is focus. Except for the first day, I found myself wanting to buy all of the systems that were available. Obviously, if I did we would be tempted to spread ourselves too thin. Some say we already are. It is much more effective to start with one idea and move on to the next. We are doing three things: Real Estate, Stocks and Inforpreneuring. That is it. Well, we are doing a little Network Marketing as well, but that is a minor thing since we have a partner helping us. The point is to stay focused and allow yourself the chance to have good things happen!

them. Practice them. Make them your strengths! You can achieve almost anything through desire and practice. You might not be able to dunk a basketball, but that shouldn't prevent you from playing the game. In business, you might not build a company like Microsoft, but you can still be successful in software with the right idea, desire and perseverance. The only thing holding you back from success is you. Practice, apply and don't give up!

Here is another exercise. Get that pencil or pen and grab your pad of paper. Draw a line down the middle of the page. In the left column, write down all the things you love to do. Do not move to the right column until you have racked your brain and listed everything. After you have exhausted your love list, make an equally comprehensive list in the right column of everything you do *not* like to do.

When you are finished with those lists, create a second divided page. Look through the lists on the first page and circle your top ten items in each column. Transfer those items to the appropriate column on the new page. Now give each item in your "like" column a numerical ranking from ten to one, with ten being your favorite. Do the same for your "dislike" column, with ten being the item you dislike most.

There were other lessons as well, but I must get focused and make phone calls on some hot Real Estate leads. While many of you already knew the things I listed here, it is important to remember that the old lessons are usually the ones we forget. For me, I am renewing my resolve to be more thoughtful about how I speak, to pay better attention to my spiritual needs and to sharpen my focus over the next five weeks.

One last thing: I have a friend I am coaching and he is really catching on to the idea of success. One of the things he is doing is "bird dogging" leads in his community for me. Could this be a business for him? People who have good research skills and a knack for finding properties, leads and prospects could sell their skills for a cut of the profit. I hope you all have a great week!

****

You can mourn the past
or you can celebrate your future!
- Roger Mallory

Check out our example:

Things You Love to Do	**Things You Don't Like to Do**
Fishing	The Stock Market
Woodworking	Managing complex projects
Surfing the net	Doing the dishes
Swimming	Cleaning the bathroom
Sketching and painting	Coding and Programming
Talking to people	Painting the house
Cooking	Repetitive tasks
Solving puzzles	Falling from high places
Flying	Sleeping on hard surfaces
Travel	Speaking in front of crowds
Good jokes	Being alone
Creating new projects	Balancing the checkbook
Running	Cleaning of any sort
Bad jokes	

Save these sheets in a notebook. Later in this book we will discuss choosing your income streams, and you will need these lists. You can use these rankings to test whether or not a potential stream is really for you. These lists will help you figure it out.

For each income stream you consider working on, figure out what qualities are necessary. Take a tally for each income stream based on the ranking you assigned each relevant quality. Enter the dislike numbers as negative and the like numbers as positive. Add the numbers together. If the total is negative, you might want to reconsider that stream.

For example, if you decide to get involved with the information delivery industry by writing a book, you need to like writing, research, grammar, proofreading, formatting documents, negotiating with a publisher, and marketing. If you like most of these aspects and give those qualities a high positive ranking that outweighs the aspects of book writing you don't like, then this income stream might be for you. If your negatives outweigh your positives, you might want to consider a different stream.

Now let's return to your passions list. Write down things you really enjoy, whether or not you have a special talent in those areas. For example, you might not sing or play an instrument, but you might really love music. Add it to the list. For everything you like but are not good at, you can learn. That adds to the excitement of changing your life.

Using your lists as a springboard, write a one- to two-page description of your ideal life. If your circumstances were perfect, what would your life be like? Be specific. Include descriptions of your car and home and other surroundings. What would you do for fun, work, etc? You will use this description as a guide to plan your new life.

When you do the planning you are going to want to put together a group of activities and possible streams that fit what you want to do. Passion is one of the keys to success along the path you choose, so when you design your program you need to remember what you love to do.

In the previous chapter we gave you a very lucrative plan for a per-

March 5, 2003
Roger's journal entry

Today's will be a fairly short entry. I played phone tag with the owner of the house I spoke about yesterday and worked on the website. We had some server problems, so I probably will not be caught up on these entries until Friday or Saturday.

I have talked to the owner of the house. It is a custom-built house designed by a famous Seattle architect. It has been enhanced quite a bit with a four-car garage and a master suite. The asking price is the bank appraisal at $550k, although he has received input from other experts that the actual value is in excess of $600k. This needs to be verified.

It is in a great neighborhood and a hot market that for the last few years has been moving up at a 7-10% clip. Roof, heat and hot water are all newer and in great condition. The grounds are well landscaped and there is a pool and a hot tub. It also comes partially furnished. It will be interesting to see what furnishings are in it.

son who loves woodworking. When you write out a plan based on your interests, you will end up with what is essentially a list of products you can offer in exchange for an income. You can use this list to develop the sources of income that reflect your uniqueness. A set of ideas and businesses you will love to do! See if you can develop a plan from your list that reflects your loves and passions.

As you work on your description of your new life, remember you have made a commitment to seriously changing and improving your life circumstances. Do not allow yourself to edit your description based on your current reality. Allow yourself to imagine your ideal life and write an honest account. You will set up the foundation of that life the *instant* you begin your Six Week Adventure, so be sure you know exactly where you are headed. The more honest you are in terms of your ideal life, the closer you will be to achieving your goals.

He seems quite interested in getting rid of it. However, he needs to be in agreement with his wife before they sell. From him I got a definite don't-want-her feeling, but his wife might not be there yet. However, he says his wife's health is not the greatest and that leads me to believe she might be ready. We will be able to tell more on Friday when I visit the house. I have tentatively scored the house a 12, though a 13 is likely pending the financing and the accuracy of the appraisal.

Get a notebook

After completing these exercises, it is time to organize them your lists and plans. Get a three-ring binder and put your worksheets into it. This will become your personal What-I-want-to-do notebook. As you read further in this book, refer back to your binder pages for clues as to what is best for you and how you want to structure your sources of income.

Prepare mentally and spiritually

Spiritual Awareness is important in this process. We believe prayer and active involvement with worship is invaluable in making a life a place of change.

Our spiritual connections have given us great support. If you do not have a formal belief system, at the very least read something inspirational on a regular basis... something that has nothing to do with your Adventure work. Allow your mind and soul a chance to recover and to stay balanced.

During our Adventure, Marita and I followed our Christian tradition to prepare ourselves mentally and spiritually. Regardless of your personal religious convictions, you can use our suggestions to prepare yourself according to your beliefs.

We did a few things we considered essential to the success of our Adventure. First, we prayed! It was very important for us to stay in touch with God on this project. For me in particular, prayer gave me the ability to keep in perspective our reasons for taking on the Six Week Adventure. Had we been motivated by greed, the Adventure would have resulted in failure. Prayer helped us stay on track and in the right frame of mind.

Secondly, we kept in touch with people who understood our spiritual state. We are fortunate to have a strong group of friends. They were a great source of comfort and advice as we went through our Adventure. These six weeks are an intense time that requires a great deal of mental and spiritual energy to keep focus. A strong support network is critical, and we will revisit the importance of this network in Chapter 6.

Lastly, we focused on giving. Part of being successful is learning to share your good fortune with others. In the Judeo-Christian traditions, ten percent is known as a tithe. Whatever you choose to call it, understand its importance to the success of your Adventure. Giving helps build passion and perspective.

If you don't have the cash, give of your time and in other ways that will benefit your favorite cause or charity. Learn to give regularly and you will be surprised at the benefits that come your way.

Now that you are prepared, now that you have a clear idea of your starting point and the resources you bring to your Six Week Adventure, you are ready to draw up a plan. The next chapter will take you one step closer to starting your Adventure.

> *Success isn't something you chase. It is something you have to put forth the effort for constantly; then maybe it'll come when you least expect it.*
> – Michael Jordan

****

Every day you may make progress.
Every step may be fruitful.
Yet there will stretch out before you
an ever-lengthening, ever-ascending,
ever-improving path.
You know you will never get
to the end of the journey.
But this, so far from discouraging,
only adds to the joy and glory of the climb.
- Sir Winston Churchill

CHAPTER 4
KEY 2: PLAN YOUR SUCCESS

To achieve happiness, we should make certain that we are never without an important goal.
– Earl Nightingale

One of the keys to success is successful thinking. This might sound circular but it is not. In ***Think and Grow Rich***, Hill suggests that you need a compelling vision and need to pursue that vision with passion. Every successful person I have ever met – and you will see this in every book I refer to – is a person who sets goals that are challenging to meet.

You've probably heard the saying: You can shoot for the stars and even if you fail, you will at least get the moon. Don't be afraid to challenge yourself with goals that are ambitious. You will achieve many more of them than you thought possible. Even the goals where you fall short will still be successful.

Every trip needs a plan. Key 2 focuses on how to put together the plan for your Adventure. While Keys 1, 3 and 4 help you determine the requirements and content of your plan, Key 2 will help you sit down and write your plan. This chapter spells out the essentials you need in order to take on the Six Week Adventure the same way we did. We will help you grasp the scope of what you will do during the weeks you set aside for your Adventure.

March 5, 2003
Marita's journal entry

As I reflect back to the prior week and the seminars, I remember one of the topics was moving out of the box and looking at other options that can arise. I find this especially true today in the area of disappointment. It is so easy to let obstacles get in the way and stop you from proceeding.

Roger and I are trying to adopt an infant. Today a roadblock occurred with the agency we are working with. It hit me hard and became a real downer but practicing the idea of going beyond the box has left Roger and me with other possibilities. We still have the dream of a family, and instead of being sad and upset I'm excited to move on.

Research, read and learn!

In his book ***The Joyful Christian***, C.S. Lewis speaks about the difference between a map and an ocean. He says that to truly experience the ocean, we need a map as well as the ocean. Though a map is just ink on paper, and you can walk in the sand beside the real thing, you can never get from New York to London by experiencing a walk in the sand. The map is the sum of the experiences of many people who have experienced the ocean, and we use it to enjoy the ocean more completely... and to get where we are going.

Likewise, we all need to learn. If your Six Week Adventure is to succeed, you must acquire a little preparatory knowledge. It is easy to learn what you need to know. You just have to gather a few essential resources and take some time to study them. I mentioned a few authors in Chapter 1 whose Writing gave us a solid foundation for setting up new sources of income. You, too, will find knowledge and inspiration from many written sources.

We would like to share with you the books we found

invaluable. We have helpful resources – books, audio course tapes and created a list of websites – in Appendix V. Remember you do not need to buy all of these books. Check with friends or your local libraries first.

While we encourage you to read and learn as much as possible before you start your Adventure, the following four books are must-reads:

Think and Grow Rich
by Napoleon Hill, Mass Market Paperback: 256 pages
Publisher: Fawcett Books
Reissue edition (November 1990); ISBN: 0449214923.

If there is one book besides ours that can help you plan for your Adventure, this is the one. Very few people understand it after the first reading. But read through it a few times and you will be amazed how much you learn.

Thou Shall Prosper: Ten Commandments for Making Money
by Rabbi Daniel Lapin, Hardcover: 362 pages
Publisher: John Wiley & Sons
1st edition (September 13, 2002); ISBN: 0471218685.

A Jewish Rabbi takes the reader through the traditional Jewish view of money. This is a great book to help understand how to deal with the destructive myths about money in modern society.

Create Your Own Future:
How to Master the 12 Critical Factors of Unlimited Success
by Brian Tracy, Hardcover: 288 pages
Publisher: John Wiley & Sons
1st edition (August 16, 2002); ISBN: 0471251070.

This is a must-read primer on success. It is well written and a quick read.

The Psychology of Persuasion: How to Persuade Others to Your Way of Thinking
by Kevin Hogan, _Hardcover: 280 pages
Publisher: Pelican Pub Co; (June 1996); ISBN: 1565541464.

This is the best book out there for learning the techniques of persuasion. Hogan is a wonderful writer. While Cialdini's book – listed in Appendix V – is more in-depth than this one, it is also more academic and much more difficult to wade through.

Of all the books we recommend, Hogan's is the easiest to read and understand. I suggest you listen to the audio version of Hogan's book. It is very well done and will allow you to hear the inflection of various phrases.

Read everything you can before you start to draw up your plan. The knowledge you gain from these resources will help you prepare ambitious yet realistic goals. The information you gather at the research stage will enable you to think creatively about how to reach those goals.

Write down all of your goals

After you read and research as much as you can, write down everything you would like to do and add this list to your notebook. You will want to check this list against your other lists to ensure you are making the right decisions. For us, this was more a series of discussions than a set process. We wrote down the things we liked doing and then decided what we wanted to do.

Regardless of what process you use to set your goals, remember these four essential points:

- Think outside the box
- Make informed decisions
- Write down your goals
- Check your goals against the work you have done so far

You want your goals to be sufficiently ambitious to help you achieve success, yet realistic enough to put into practice. Use your goal setting process to look for opportunities that will maximize your time and hold your interest. See Appendix II for a goal setting process you can follow.

Determining your goals will be faster and more focused than the personal assessments you made in the previous chapter. You will want to narrow the list of possibilities and have specific goals in mind. At this stage, you are looking for a concrete starting point and you are ready to draw up the actual plan for your Adventure. You will want to have things in writing.

The most critical decision we made was to set our goals higher than we thought we could reach. We wrote down goals that would lead to our first million within six months. When we decided to focus on Real Estate as one of our income streams, we set our sights on the purchase of a total of $500, 000 in Real Estate during our Adventure. This seemed ambitious at first... until we bought one house that is worth $600, 000! With ambitious goals, you maximize opportunity.

Make a plan

Now that you have assessed your situation, brainstormed and drawn up a list of goals, it won't take long for you to draft a written plan. First, you need to write a statement of purpose for your Adventure. Then you need a Business Action Plan for each

income stream you will pursue. Each plan should be a page or less. Just get the basics down. You can always add to it or modify it later.

Each Business Action Plan should be structured as follows:

- **Statement of Purpose:** What stream of income will you pursue and how will you pursue it?
- **Specific Goals:** What will be the specific outcome of your efforts in

March 6, 2003

Roger's journal entry

I am committed to spending Thursdays in Olympia, Washington. It is a place where property values are seeing a healthy appreciation and at the same time affordability is still there. My two main objectives today were to talk with a Real Estate agent and get my friend Steve to "bird dog" for me on some discount mortgages.

We went to the courthouse and it was quite easy to find the mortgage information we were looking for. Steve is a great sales person and researcher and I believe he will do very well at this part of our Real Estate business.

After a quick lunch, we visited a Real Estate agent and met for the first time with Steve's choice for an agent. This one is a home run! This guy knows the investment world and holds property himself. He has a good grasp of what is going on in his community and is not threatened by us going after deals he is

this area by the end of your Adventure?

- **First-Three-Actions List:** What are the first three steps you will take to get started? This is an important step to get the process going. Three items are enough to give you a powerful kick-start. Ready, Fire, Aim! Here's an example:

- **Statement of Purpose:** I plan to pursue Real Estate Investing by purchasing "ugly" houses and reselling them.
- **Specific Goals:** I will buy six houses per year using no-money-down owner-carry-back strategies. I will obtain a minimum net profit of $15, 000 per house.
- **Specific Methods:** I will search newspaper adds for flexible sellers and identify 10-15 each week. I will seek out FSBO's and ugly houses by driving around. I will make a minimum of 15 calls per week to flexible buyers and follow up with old listings every two weeks. I will use investors for the first two purchases to establish a track record. I will enlist friends to clean up properties. I will sell the houses via signs and newspaper adds.
- **First-Three-Actions List:** I will get the Sunday paper on the first Sunday of the Adventure and identify the flexible seller ads. On the same day I will respond to five ads and assess the properties. I will make an appointment to visit one of the houses and talk to the owner.

Keep your Business Action Plan short and finish it quickly. It's important not to let this stage of prepara-

not involved with. He is a definite winner and will be a great addition to the team.

After I came home, I did some homework on Robert Allen and John Childers's stuff. I reviewed sections on creative financing and structuring deals. Tomorrow, I go look at the 550k house.

Another deal may be in play as well. The duplex Steve lives in might be for sale. I will have to do the homework, but at the asking price it appears there is a positive cash flow. More on this one over the weekend.

One thing I forgot to mention in my entry last night was a meeting my friend Roy and I had with a larger group of our friends about wealth building. Roy did most of the talking and the guys appeared interested in what we were doing. I think Roy now has the vision of where these things can take him.

tions slow you down or encourage you to procrastinate. This should be a rapid-fire means for you to plan and take action as soon as you start your Adventure. And this step will move you that much closer to your start date.

Establish your timeframe

As soon as you draft your Business Action Plan for each income stream, you are ready to nail down the timeframe for your Adventure. As discussed in the previous chapter, six weeks is the ideal minimum. It allows enough time to ensure a reasonable amount of success yet it's short enough to create a sense of urgency. The Six Week Adventure requires focus and discipline.

Distractions will arise, but your plan should be designed to keep you on track and to minimize the temptation to procrastinate.

Six weeks is compatible with many severance packages and educational leaves. If you don't have six weeks available to set up your new income streams, your goal right now will be to prepare for when you can arrange time to take this Adventure.

Now that you are prepared to start your Adventure, you will want to establish and focus on an actual start date. If you are still employed, you will need to make arrangements to secure your time off. You still

March 7, 2003
Marita's journal entry

The art of giving, a concept rallied in the seminars is truly more of a blessing to the giver than the receiver. On Friday mornings I teach two and three year olds while their mothers attend a Bible study at our church. It is one of the highlights of my week. These children are so loving and caring. We just have a ball in class: singing, talking and playing while we learn about Jesus.

While visiting Disney World during our trip to Orlando, I picked up some compact washcloths that expand once they hit water. Each towel has a different Disney character. At the end of the day I gave each child a washcloth. The response from these children was amazing. They were so thrilled. They couldn't believe I gave them each a gift, much less one with Mickey Mouse and Pooh and other characters on it. One boy kept saying how nice I was.

I left that day so blessed. It was great to see grins on children's faces because they were thought of. I'd like to find more ways to put smiles on other people's faces.

have more preparatory work to do, and we will discuss that in the next two chapters. By setting a date now, you will be compelled to move quickly through the rest of the preparations.

Get feedback from mentors

In the next chapter we discuss how to set up a support network and acquire mentors. It's best if you discuss your Business Action Plans with your mentors. Their feedback will prove invaluable. By gathering their suggestions before you begin your Adventure, you will have a better chance to modify your goals or action steps accordingly.

A mentor can help you on this in a number of ways. While you are encouraged to go forward with your goals, your mentor can help you remain grounded. You can get from your mentor a real sense of what the day-to-day grind will be like. S/he can also point to things that might be troublesome. For example, you will not typically be listed high in search engines overnight. That process can take weeks or even months, and that's the type of realistic understanding you need to start with even as you aim for your ambitious goals. Look to your mentor to help you understand your business.

CHAPTER 5
KEY 3: SET UP YOUR DREAM TEAM

Destiny is not a matter of chance; it is a matter of choice.
– Anonymous

A successful Six Week Adventure is not the product of one person's efforts. In this chapter we talk about the importance and process of developing relationships with key people. These people will be essential to the success of your Adventure and will play critical roles over the longer term. We address the roles of 11 different types of people with the power to bring you greater success. These people comprise your First Team and your Second Team.

Think back to the Simon and Garfunkel song, "I am a Rock, " which is a parody of going it alone. No one becomes successful alone. The greats of industry, business and politics have always achieved success because they assembled a team of people they could rely on. They also had mentors! To succeed in your Six Week Adventure, you will need your own team and mentors.

You can't gather your support team without networking. If you don't have substantial networks already in place, this chapter will offer suggestions as to where you can start. One rule of networking is that it should have been done yesterday. Depressing, I know, but don't worry. You still have time to assemble your team. Just don't wait any longer. Get started today!

March 7, 2003
From Roger
Today I did a lot of study and review. This was my first tour of a house with what I hoped was a pre-qualified "don't-want-her." And he was. It was very clear he wants to be out of the house. His wife was not present, however.

One of the best things I think John Childers ever said was to learn to shut up! As we toured the house, all I had to do was ask a few short questions and he would go on with all the information.

At the end, I asked about the financing and I was surprised at how easily he went to the point of carrying back 80% of the contract and then quickly backed off to an even lower amount on the down. It seems reasonable that I could get a 10-15% down with owner financing here. This actually raised the score to a 13. This house is spectacular!

One of the really cool things was that this gentleman was an incredibly nice guy and he knows Real Estate very well. This is one of those situations where win-win is really cool. I want a great deal but it will be

Your First Team

Your spouse

Function: Moral support and personal grounding. All manner of decision-making and encouragement will come from your spouse.

Your spouse, if you have one, will play an important role in your Adventure. If your spouse is not interested or is against the idea, you can find ways to invest in new income streams without his or her direct support. But if your spouse is behind you on this Adventure, you will find the process much easier. The six weeks is a concentrated effort that works best with a couple in agreement.

Most financial advisors suggest each spouse should have a separate strategy and take care of his or her piece of the pie. If your spouse is at least passively supportive, you can move forward with your Adventure and pursue income streams for which you have a personal affinity.

The process will work much better, however, if your spouse participates actively. Whether or not your spouse sets up his or her own income stream, it will be helpful if s/he participates at least in the savings and budget decisions.

If you and your spouse experience disagreement on whether or not to pursue the Six Week Adventure, the primary difference is probably over the issue of money. If this is the case, it is time to seek a good counselor. Money, according to most polls, is the number one problem at the center of divorce. During my days as a pastor, I learned that one of the keys to a strong, lasting marriage was a unified approach toward how money is handled. Without agreement on money, the Six Week Adventure will be difficult for a couple to negotiate.

with a nice seller! One other thing is that they went to the same church I did a number of years ago. We have common acquaintances. This seemed to set him somewhat at ease.

Now it's time for Marita to see the house and for us to meet his wife. Maybe we can go over there on Sunday afternoon. This might be our first one! I just need to keep my wits and stay unemotional about it.

Marita and I believe in the importance of the marriage partnership, so we were very much of one mind in the way we approached our Six Week Adventure. Because we had different strengths and interests, we focused on different income streams to complement and reinforce each other's efforts. Through our partnership, we moved much more quickly toward our goals than we would have done solo.

Trusted friends who understand what you are doing

Function: Additional moral support. Cheap labor – don't abuse this. Expert advice if they are able. Great to celebrate with!

Friends who support you on your Adventure will help you achieve success. Their moral support will be critical when you face obstacles. And if they decide to become involved in the process, they might prove to be valuable contacts, mentors or partners. They will offer new perspectives and suggestions as well as encouragement.

If you have friends who are not supportive, consider whether or not they are really friends. Sometimes these people are just acquaintances and it might be time to move on. If their friendship means a lot to you and they do not support your Adventure, just focus on what you are doing and don't discuss your projects much with them.

We have a number of good friends who were somewhat skeptical. We sat down with them and explained the issues and our objectives. After that, we gave them regular updates. We briefed them on what we had accomplished and showed them the concrete results of our ongoing projects. Now most of them are on board in pursuit of their own projects and two are doing exceptionally well.

Don't be deterred by anyone's skepticism. If you keep your focus and have faith in what you are doing, the naysayers either join the parade or disappear. Most importantly, focus on your friendships with people who are supportive. You will help each other in the process.

Your banker

Function: Notary, Checking and Savings, and other banking services. Many banks offer loan services for business, personal and/or Real Estate. A good banker can give advice on other things – such as Stocks, if s/he has a broker association.

Most likely you have a relationship with a bank already. To make the most of your Adventure, you will need to take some time to get to know the bankers in your local branch. They can prove to be a valuable asset in the process of setting up new income streams. Depending on the streams you choose, you might opt to take out a loan of some type. Your banker is there for that service. I would advise using a smaller local bank for these kinds of things.

If you are uncomfortable using your existing bank for your investments, ask trusted friends and associates for their recommendations. Often the best finance professionals are discovered through word of mouth. You might also check with a local chamber of commerce or similar business support organization.

If you decide to find a new financial institution, consider interviewing several bankers before you select your new bank. Keep in mind the criteria most important to you and to the projects you will engage in on your Adventure. Be candid when you interview bankers, as they can be very helpful.

You might want to consider using more than one bank. We have a relationship with four different institutions for different business and investment purposes. For our primary bank, we wanted a medium-small bank where we would get a bit more flexibility. We took a recommendation from my parents and that bank turned out to be the best one for us.

When you interview bankers, come prepared with a list of questions that address your immediate and long-term objectives. Find out what services they offer that you might need down the road, such as merchant card services.

March 10, 2003 –
Marita's journal entry

Today my focus has been on the Stock market. I've been listening to the tapes and reading. I started my paper trading. I have purchased one call option on Hershey and two puts that will need to be traded by Friday, March 21. I also purchased three other puts. Let's see how I do in a week from now.

****

A happy person is not a person
in a certain set of circumstances,
but rather a person
with a certain set of attitudes.
– Hugh Downs

You need a banker who will help you grow your income streams and address all your long-term needs. This might not seem important to you now. But remember, when you set up your income streams and things get rolling, your life will change. You need to plan now so that you have the support team you need in place when your income streams start to grow.

Mortgage Broker and Real Estate agent

Function: Facilitate Real Estate investment stream. Your banker might make the mortgage broker unnecessary. And you might not need a Real Estate agent. It depends on your goals and situation.

If you plan to focus on Real Estate investment, it is critical that you take the time to call around and interview mortgage brokers. As with bankers, you should start with referrals by friends and associates. Next you might try the local Real Estate club. Find out if they work with investors and then find out if they invest in Real Estate.

We discovered our mortgage broker through my Real Estate calls. The broker was working with one of our investors to help sell a property. After a productive conversation, I was certain this broker was someone I wanted to deal with. He turned out to be great!

Real Estate agents are tough and it's best to avoid them. Sometimes you need them, though. You can find agents through the same process you use to find a broker. Interview many before you make your selection. Ask if they are flexible on the terms they offer. Will they let you meet the seller? If they are not willing to help you do these things, look further.

You will often be told there is a certain way things are done and that some things you cannot do. This is simply not true. If you decide to set up a Real Estate income stream, you will learn that you must keep options open.

When you discover an agent relationship that works, it is pure gold! We have yet to find an agent we want to work with forever, but we do have a friend who is new to the business. Our hope is that she will become this flexible kind of agent.

Before you interview an agent or broker, prepare a list of questions that will help you determine if that person can really provide the level of professional support you need. If you focus on Real Estate as one of your income streams, each member of your financial team should be a Real Estate investor. They must also have substantial experience and knowledge of local markets.

Mentors

Function: To advise and encourage you in your ventures. They are also there to help and warn you about possible pitfalls. These are the people who have gone before you and are now ready to encourage you on your way.

Mentors are the final members of your First Team but that doesn't mean you should look for them last. Mentors will help you at all stages of your Adventure, including the preparations stage, so you'll want to keep your eyes open for them from the beginning. An old saying suggests that when the student is ready, the teacher will appear. Now that you are ready, look around and see where your mentors might be.

If your family and friends are supportive, start with them. Some will make great mentors. They might also be more willing than strangers to provide names of acquaintances that can help. Friends and family will take you only so far. If you need more mentors, here are some great places to continue your search:

- SCORE is an organization of retired business people set up specifically to help small businesses and entrepreneurs. We have not worked with them but have spoken to people who have used their services and commented favorably. It is worth your time to contact this organization. They have chapters in almost every major city.

- Local organizations such as Kiwanis Clubs, Chambers of Commerce and City Leagues are wonderful places to get to know people.

- Specialized groups such as Toastmasters, the YMCA, Real Estate and Investment Clubs are very friendly and well worth visiting.

- Churches or other places of worship offer a great environment to seek out mentors and other team members. Here you will find like-minded people who can give you good leads to other professionals that share your ethical perspectives.

- Your child's PTA is also a good place to meet business professionals in a safe, neutral setting.

Making initial contact with these organizations is not enough. You will need to reach out and network with individual members. Not everybody is an extrovert and you might not have much experience or confidence in your ability to cultivate mentor relationships. But if you are going to succeed in your Adventure, you need to take this opportunity to learn to step out and meet people. If you are concerned about your ability to do this, here are three steps that will help you achieve your goal of networking and finding suitable mentors:

- **Take a more extroverted, experienced or confident friend with you**
  Ask them to establish initial contact. Allow them to coach you through your fears.

- **Read the Kevin Hogan book, *Psychology and Persuasion* recommended in the previous chapter**
  When you master effective communication, you will find it much easier to get to know people. You will approach new contacts with greater confidence.

- **Start with safe places**
  Ask your church pastor to make introductions. SCORE is also a safe means of contact, because it allows you to speak to a mentor one-on-one, as you would a dentist or doctor. It is a prearranged conversation rather than an open-ended social event in which you need to reach out and meet people.

When you seek your mentors, remember that the type of mentor is not as nearly as important as the character of the mentor. Investment and entrepreneurial activities are so much easier if you work and consult with someone you can trust and confide in. That is the essence of mentoring and should be the basis for choosing your primary mentors.

If you need additional mentors with specialized skills, you can purchase that service from a number of sources. Nearly every guru offers a mentorship program. We offer a similar program available through our website at **http://www.anbeyond.com/courses/courses.html**.

But wherever possible, try to find mentors locally. Someone you can meet for coffee or a round of golf. Someone who can provide immediate, face-to-face feedback and support, who can be a visible presence in your life. I have two such mentors: Dian Thomas, and Rick, a very successful trade show promoter in our area. The right type of mentor is invaluable to the success of your Adventure.

****

Take the first Step in faith.
You don't have to see the whole staircase.
Just take the first step.
- Martin Luther King Jr.

Your Second Team

New friends

Function: New friends are your new contacts, future partners and possible future mentors. As you venture farther along your envisioned path to the future, the people you meet will have much more in common with what you are doing. They will become part of what you are trying to achieve.

When you pursue networking opportunities, you will meet people interested in your Adventure. They might be on a similar Adventure and able to provide a sounding board to discuss challenges. You can share your experiences with them. Don't hesitate to cultivate these relationships. You will receive positive reinforcement and learn things that can help you reach your goals successfully.

We have met so many fine people. Included in that list are a number of people who have now shifted to mentor status and still others who are just interested in what we are doing. The one that comes to mind at this time is Dian Thomas at **http://www.dianthomas.com.** If you don't remember Dian from NBC's *Today* some years back, you are in for a real treat just by visiting her website. We met Dian at a seminar we attended to learn about the seminar business. Dian is a wonderful person and has been very gracious in helping me with this book and my fledgling business.

Remember that you can network in a number of places. Look for groups and events that are of interest to you, whether or not these have direct bearing on your planned income streams. Anyone you meet

March 11, 2003
Roger's journal entry

We had some rather difficult stuff happen today. We have reached a snag in our adoption process and both Marita and I have taken it pretty hard. We are taking most of the day off. We did meet with the broker today and he thinks we can do something with a mortgage on the house. Other than that, we took most of the day and spent it dealing with our personal stuff.

might prove to be a great business contact, whether or not the conversation starts out in that direction. Carry business cards with you to all events, just in case. You will meet wonderful people! Don't miss the opportunity and the privilege to have the joy of good friends.

March 12, 2003 Marita's journal entry

Being around positive people is the best medicine for the "I feel sorry for me" blues. I went to my Bible Study and then later to help serve food for the parents and children who participate in Awana's at church. A big crowd was there. Many smiling faces greeted us on "backwards night." The food line started with dessert and everyone wore their clothes backwards.

It was just the humor I needed after yesterday's feelings of gloom and doom. Roger and I believe the setback on an adoption is just that: a setback. We are moving forward on what needs to be done. It feels a whole lot better doing something than just being upset and feeling put upon.

Possible partners

Function: Business in its most essential form is about people and what they bring to its success. If your business has a need you can't fulfill, partners fill in the gaps. Often these are people you know already. But just as many will come from relationships you will build in the future.

Partnerships are critical to your success, but they should never be total partnerships. Instead, you should look for mutually beneficial ways to cooperate on specific projects with limited terms. Always create a legal agreement on the nature and limits of the partnership. The following websites are great resources for the legal aspects of partnerships:

www.secretmillionaire.com
www.legalees.com

We partner on everything except Stock investing. In one example, we are partnering with my father on Real Estate investing. We paid the fee for him to attend a seminar on Tax Liens and he is fast learning the Real Estate investment business. Now we can cover twice the ground and combine our strengths on this one stream, yet the other streams do not enter into this relationship.

As you establish plans for your Adventure, consider

what ingredients might be missing. Wherever you lack something to make each stream successful, think about who you might bring in as a partner. What are your relative strengths? Do you have friends or acquaintances with complementary strengths? Friends who might be supportive and interested in joining you on this Adventure? Your answers to these questions will be an important part of your plans.

Let's consider an example. Perhaps you are interested in Real Estate investing. You have strong credit and a knack for finding great properties. You have no ability to make a down payment, however, and the owner doesn't want to carry back the down. It is time to find a partner who has some money and wants a better return on it. Perhaps your potential partner has no feel for what constitutes a good Real Estate investment or no time to search for properties, but you do. Combine your resources, share your strengths and accomplish your mutual goals.

If you decide one or more partnerships will help you succeed on your Adventure, be very clear as to what you require in a partner. Outline the criteria before you start your search. Keep the discussions candid and focused. Plan to stay the majority partner, except in three special situations:

Every Obstacle an Opportunity

This column is going to be a little different than others I have written. This one is much more close to my heart and comes out of something traumatic that happened to my wife and me yesterday. We hit a major roadblock in our adoption process and it is very difficult to handle. To be accurate, I should say the first half of the day was tough! The rest of the day was very encouraging and that is what I want to talk to you about.

First, we went to my mortgage broker's office to talk to him about the house we are buying. This was the first time Marita met him and she immediately liked him. In the midst of the conversation, we discovered he attended a church I was familiar with. This solidified the feeling that he was the right guy to work with.

Then we went to see the Adult Ministry Pastor at our church to talk with him about what happened that morning. It was a very encouraging time and we left feeling much better. Early in the evening, we received a call from our church's senior pastor and he

- You can split the partnership equally if you have a *really* exceptional trust between you and the other partner. In the case of our partnership with my father, we were willing to go 50/50. I trust my father because of his substantial business background... and I always know where to find him!

- You can begin an equal partnership in a small and limited venture with a student or someone who wants to learn from your expertise – someone who wants you for a mentor. I partnered with my friend Steve in his Network Marketing venture. Steve is learning a great deal and the risk for me is very limited.

- If you have cash that you are willing to invest as a passive minority, you might gain substantial returns without majority involvement. Perform a thorough due diligence and invest carefully, of course. Never settle for anything less than a *very* significant return in this type of situation.

Partnerships are always taxing but can be very beneficial if planned carefully. If you enter into a passive partnership, be certain that partner really understands his or her role will be passive. If you plan to work

asked us to join them for dinner at their home Thursday evening. It was a very good end to a very rough day.

Just a side note here: regardless of your religious tradition, it is important to have support in the spiritual areas of your life. Even if you don't have a bit of religion in you, surround yourself with people whose wisdom you trust. You will need them when the road gets rocky!

So why did I share all of this? Because we were able to put into practice a key principle we have learned:

Every obstacle presents an opportunity!

If we had stopped our day after encountering the "roadblock, " we would not have found out that our Mortgage Broker was a "church going guy, " something Marita and I were thrilled with. It would not have occurred to us to take time to go to lunch and enjoy each other's company. We would not have gone to see our pastor and receive the encouragement and uplifting that he gave us. In short, we were shocked into taking care of ourselves in the the midst of the intense effort of these six weeks! This

with active partners, make sure you can get along personally. Take the time to understand your potential partners' attitudes towards money. As with your spouse, the closer you and your partner are in your philosophical approach to money, the smoother the partnership will be.

Lawyer

Function: Legal representation and opinion. Always helpful in situations where contracts are involved.

You need to select lawyers experienced in the areas in which you plan to work. If you plan to concentrate on Real Estate investing, your lawyer must be experienced in the various nuances of Real Estate law. Check with your local Real Estate club and Bar Association. As with the other professionals who will help you on this Adventure, you should plan to interview several candidates. If a lawyer wants to charge you for the 15 minutes it takes to get your questions answered, move on to another person. You want a lawyer who wants your business!

Local business contacts

Function: Marketing is more than advertising. It is about finding people to help you get your product or service in circulation. Who better to start with than the local business contacts you make? They are also a good source of mentors and future partners.

afternoon was opportunity number one. Now we have opportunity number two! I have seldom taken the time in recent years to sit and talk with a pastor from our local church. As a result of this "roadblock, " I will now have several meetings with this wonderful and wise man. What an opportunity! I am a "wanna become a better man and husband" junky and I know after these sessions, I will be! Talk about a super blessing!

Folks, every time you stumble and every time a traumatic change occurs in your life, you have a choice. You can either let it defeat you and stymie your efforts or you can look for the opportunity and use it to strengthen your resolve. When you pursue your dreams, when you are after the goals you have set in you life, know that you will encounter obstacles. Some will be large and others smaller, but all of them can get in your way. Don't let them! Defeat them by seizing the opportunities they present!

We are choosing to seize the opportunities and move on with our lives and our goals. We hope you will too when the time arrives!

You will want to join the various Chambers of Commerce, Rotary Clubs and other associations relevant to your chosen income streams.

Business contacts are essential to the growth of any business. Here are some websites to start with:

www.2chambers.com
www.uschamber.com
www.bbb.com
www.rotary.org
www.toastmasters.org
www.businessnation.com

There are many other local business fraternities and specialized clubs you can join. Ask around and you will most likely receive an invitation to some of these organizations.

People who offer specialized services

Function: Depending on the income streams you pursue, you will need the services of one of more of the following:

- **Escrow /Real Eatate Lawyer:** Eventually you will need a one or both of these people if you choose Real Estate as one of your streams. Legal advice is cheap compared to making an expensive mistake. The best place to find one of these professionals is via a mortgage broker or a local Real Estate club.

- **Stock Trading Guru and Stock Broker:** Contrary to a lot of the wisdom out there, the Stock Market is one of the best ways to assure yourself of long-term gains on your investment. Evaluate the courses and information carefully when it comes to this stream. Learn to understand how these things fit into your overall plan and what your risk tolerance is. After learning from your Stock Guru, consult your broker. Somewhere between the advice of the two lies the truth.

- **Multilevel Up Line:** If you choose to do a multilevel system, evaluate the up line you have available to you. This is important and you will be very profitable if you choose wisely. Check out Daren Falter's website at **www.networkmarketingonthenet.com**. This is a great place to start. This information will help you evaluate what you will need if you decide to do Network Marketing as one of your streams.

- **Marketing and Publicity Experts:** If you plan to write a book or work on some other stream that involves publicity, learn about marketing. In fact, learn about marketing, period. I recommend two books as starting places: ***Guerrilla Marketing: Secrets for Making Big Profits from Your Small Business*** by Jay Conrad Levinson, et al, and ***Guerrilla Publicity: Hundreds of Sure-Fire Tactics to Get Maximum Sales for Minimum Dollars*** by Jill Lublin, et al. A great place to start! Then, find gurus and mentors. I can recommend two folks here. For marketing, you will be very hard-pressed to do any better than Denise Michaels: **www.denisemichaels.com**. For publicity, Dian Thomas's stuff is fantastic and can be found at: **www.milliondollarpr.com**. This list is a good starting point. Keep looking and you will find others. These experts can help you do your very best when it comes to setting up your team.

****

Industry is a better horse to ride than genius.
- Walter Lippmann

CHAPTER 6
KEY 4: GETTING IT ALL TOGETHER FOR LIFTOFF

Stretch your vision. See what can be, not just what is. Practice adding value to things, to people and to yourself.
- David Schwartz

In this chapter we discuss all the pragmatic steps that are missing from most investment, business and entrepreneurial books. We talk about important items you need to get started in your Adventure, such as business licenses and bank accounts, and we provide tips on how best to procure these items. We also discuss logistics and how to take the final steps to set your Adventure in motion.

Get the necessary documents

You need just a few documents to get started on your Adventure. If you plan to focus on Real Estate or some other type of investment strategy, you need nothing more than your various worksheets. Each investment vehicle requires its own documentation. In Real Estate, it is a good idea to have a form you can use to make offers. You might have a sellers' form among others. Most Real Estate investment books, home study courses and websites offer these forms.

You do not need a business license to start within the investment arena. That will change after you start to make money. Incorporation is a good way to preserve and protect your assets. After you have done the research on incorporating, you will want to line up a lawyer and accountant. The following websites, run by competent lawyers, are two good places to start:

www.secretmillionaire.com
www.legalees.com

We decided to obtain a business license and incorporate for liability and tax reasons. When you own or rent out property or have any substantial net worth, you are a target. The correct corporate structure will cover you where a sole proprietorship does not. Also, capital gains and other taxes can eat up a very large portion of your profit unless you protect yourself. The decision must be yours and we cannot offer legal or accounting advice. But these are the reasons we chose this route.

If you plan to do any retailing, you will need a federal tax ID. You can obtain one easily when you get your business license. Depending on where you live, you

March 13, 2003
Roger's journal entry

I spent most of the day in Olympia, WA with my buddy Steve. He has been looking at all kinds of stuff. I think much of the world now looks different to him. Like me, he is in a pretty dead-end job. We looked at some possibilities for his future.

One of the lessons I have learned throughout the first three weeks is that there is an order to things. There is a lot of hard work and long hours. Planning, testing, revising, more planning, executing, testing.... and on and on and on... It is hard to wait. We want that first deal. We want to get that income going and quit our job so we can do more of the cool creative stuff. Ah, it is a lot of hard work!

But I do love it. I really feel as though I have found a place where I can be productive and contribute in a very positive way!

We had dinner with our pastor's family this evening. They were very kind and served a wonderful dish of halibut and some incredible salad. We then went to our small group meeting. What a great group of people! They are very special, all of them.

might need a local as well as a state license. You might also need to check zoning and other restrictions regarding your home office. It is also advisable to consult with an accountant to determine what forms need to be filed, such as sales tax.

Set up any necessary accounts

We set up a business account only. We did not need to do much else, though we will shortly. A business account is fairly easy to open, provided you have the necessary qualifications. Most banks require a business license number that you will have as soon as you establish your company. In the interim you can open a second personal account that you designate for business purposes. Most business accounts have the same fee structures as private accounts, though some require minimum balances.

You will receive better service if you open your business account at the same bank you use for personal banking. If you decide to use a different bank for business transactions, consider opening an extra personal account at that bank. The superior service is usually worth maintaining the extra personal account. The bank doesn't need to know you keep your real personal account at another institution.

Get a debit card with Visa or MasterCard privileges for your business account. Be sure to guard it and understand it is not credit. It draws directly from your bank account.

Then decide whether or not you want to obtain a business credit card. Assuming you have only one credit card for personal use, you can open a second credit card account in your name and use it exclusively for business transactions. Do not obtain a second credit card if you are not well disciplined in using credit cards. The purpose of the Six Week Adventure is to help you increase your income, not your debt.

Finally, you might want to get a merchant account that allows you to accept credit cards from paying customers. If you plan to do business via the Internet, you will need two accounts: one for live point of sales and the other for Internet orders. These accounts have limits and you need to watch them carefully or you can get into trouble. You can obtain accounts from your banker or via Internet vendors. You can also get a merchant account through Costco if you are an Executive member.

If you are planning to do Internet sales, you might want to look into services such as **www.paypal.com**, a system that acts as what I call an in-between processor. Higher cost systems such as **www.2checkout.com** will also do the work for you in the event you are unable to get a regular merchant account. Most of these systems have faster setup times as well. Both of these services allow you to set up in one day, whereas a regular account can take several weeks.

Obtaining a merchant account can be a hassle but the procedure is similar to applying for a credit card. The process involves paperwork and wait time, but you should have no trouble finding a service that meets your needs. The most difficult work comes after you are approved for the account. You need to keep track of all transactions with good, accurate accounting. Keep your paperwork up-to-date and you will be in good shape.

Merchant accounts have two fees you will need to consider: a yearly or quarterly fee and transaction fee. Just as with credit cards, the yearly or quarterly fee varies from one vendor and account type to the next. If your credit is strong, you can shop around. If not, go with the best deal you can find and periodically evaluate other vendors as your credit improves.

The transaction fee is a primary source of income for credit card companies. These fees range from 1.5-10 percent per transaction from what I have found in my research. You can't get around it, but you can shop around and look for the best rate possible.

When you have your paperwork and accounts in place, you will be nearly ready to begin your Adventure. Just a few more steps remain.

Set up a journal

Now that you have created your notebook, you probably realize I am big on the idea of documenting your Adventure. I believe documenting everything is important for two reasons. First, it is a great way to stay organized and focused. Writing down what you are doing and what you have done is a fantastic way to work through the distractions and concentrate on the task at hand. Second, I believe we should have a sense of history as to who and what we are. You will be able to look back at all you have accomplished and know that a lot of good has come from your efforts.

I strongly suggest you start a daily journal and idea book. Every day, write something. We did it electronically at **http://www.anbeyond.com/sixweeks/dailyreport/index.htm**. You don't have to make a website out of your journal as we did, but get your experience down in words. You will be glad for it in the days to come.

I would also suggest you write down your inventions, ideas, creations and business opportunities in a notebook. I did this separately because I didn't want to share things that might be an advantage to me or that were not yet mature ideas. If you keep your journal personal, you can combine them into one volume. If you choose to share your journal, it is better to keep them separate.

Create your routine

Where will you be at the end of your Six Week Adventure? Remember when I asked you to future in specific dimensions? Put that vision to work when you plan your six-week schedule. Develop a daily routine that reflects your lifestyle goals and put it into writing. This will help you use the six weeks to truly achieve the lifestyle you want for yourself.

The old axiom, "Fake it 'til you make it" holds a lot of truth. What you do is what you are. If you practice what you seek, you will become it. When you devise a daily schedule that mirrors your ideal lifestyle, when you write down your routine in advance for the entire six weeks, you will get the most out of your Adventure.

Be sure to include time for work, exercise, personal responsibilities and free time. Don't forget to include the kids in this. Be realistic with your time allotments. Remember: vision and balance are the keys to a successful routine.

We wanted a balance between our income stream projects and our private lives. We also wanted to live healthier. I lost 15 pounds during the six weeks because of my healthier lifestyle. This was as much a result of our Adventure as our new sources of income.

March 13, 2003
Marita's journal entry

We had dinner with our pastor and his wife. That was great. Good food, fresh halibut and uplifting support from them.
I feel so blessed by the number of people who are encouraging us through the roadblocks we have encountered with the adoption. We are moving on.

When you write out the daily routine for your Adventure, also take the time to put a budget into place. We developed a budget based on categories created by T. Harve Eker of Peak Performance – **www.peakpotentials.com/.** These are great guidelines. Following is a sample budget. The percentages on the left are Eker's recommendations. The percentages on the right reflect the budget we created:

Long-term investing fund	10%	10%
Savings for specific purposes, e.g., new car	10%	10%
Education	10%	7%
Giving	5-10%	10%
Fun and recreation	10%	8%
Basic Needs	50-55%	55%

When you have your daily schedule and budget down on paper, start to put your routine into place a little at a time in the weeks and days leading up to your start date. It is important that this routine be as second nature as possible by the time your Adventure begins.

Establish your down time

The Six Week Adventure is very intense and you will need down time. You need to plan ahead and schedule sufficient free time. The harder you work, the more important your free time will be.

Socrates said, "The unexamined life is not worth living." A corollary would be that "the un-recreated life is the root of much misery." Do not short-change yourself. One of the most important lessons you will learn from your Adventure is that humans exist for more than the struggle to survive. Your free time is a priority.

If your Adventure is a full-time endeavor as ours was, it is advisable to schedule your free time and recreation first then schedule all other things around it. This will not only ensure you work at peak performance during your Adventure. It will also serve as a reminder that you have the power to change your lifestyle. ...to live a healthier, fuller, more rewarding life on *your* terms. That you and your family come first.

Scheduling the part-time Adventure

The Six Week Adventure is a full-time effort. It is the time and space required to put new systems into place. If you have been laid off and can put your severance package to work, or if you have vacation or leave time available, it is important that you create a full-time schedule for your Adventure – including your down time.

What if you are still working and can't take time off? Can you create a new lifestyle for yourself just by setting up new income streams in your spare time?

You have two options available. As we discussed in Chapter 4, you can try to take on this Adventure part-time on a limited scale and at a slower pace. Or you can read, research and learn in preparation for a time when you are able to devote a full six weeks to your Adventure. Because the Adventure will be more difficult as a part-time effort, we strongly recommend you rule out all other possibilities first.

If you decide to take the part-time route, here are some suggestions that might help:

- **Set aside six or more consecutive weeks to devote part of your time to your Adventure.** During the week, spend one hour a night on your Adventure. Be disciplined to do this every night, but resist the temptation to work more than an hour at a time. It's important not to cut into your down time.

- **For your weekends, find a place where you can retreat and work undisturbed for two to three hours each day.** Reserve the rest of your weekends for family and recreational activities.

- **Focus only on one income stream.** You will not have time for more than this. When you get this stream set up, you can arrange another six weeks to set up another.
- **Before you start your part-time Adventure, consider bringing in a partner who has time to do some of the work.** You need to choose a partner you really trust, someone as enthusiastic as you are. With a partner you might be tempted to take on more than one stream. Don't do this until you think very carefully about the commitment this entails. It's probably best to wait until you set up one stream before you move on to another... even with a partner.

****

Believe in yourself! Have faith in your abilities!
Without a humble but reasonable confidence
in your own powers, you cannot be successful or happy.
- Norman Vincent Peale

- **If you aren't certain you can do the Adventure part time in just six weeks, you can schedule a longer period, up to three months.** You can schedule the actual number of hours you would spend if you could devote six full-time weeks to the process. You will move at a slower pace but you will get the benefit of the full Adventure and a glimpse as to what your long-term involvement with new income streams will be like. Because your Adventure will stretch over a longer period of time, however, you will need extra discipline to stick with it. You will need to keep your schedule and goals a real priority.

Whichever part-time path you choose, be careful that you don't work on your Adventure while you're on company time. Exercising integrity and highly ethical behavior is essential to your success. As you move into the world of small business, you will discover how much success rides on your personal integrity and your word. Protect it jealously now and your future will be a lot easier.

****

Be creative.
Use unconventional thinking.
And have the guts to carry it out.
- Lee Iaccoca

CHAPTER 7
SEVEN SECRETS TO USING THE FOUR KEYS

The best thing about the future is
that it comes only one day at a time.
- Abraham Lincoln

Excellence is not a destination; it is a continuous journey
– Brian Tracy

With any endeavor you'll find right and wrong ways to do things. Here we offer six secrets that will help you plan your Six Week Adventure the right way. Our advice in this chapter will help you use your four "success keys" correctly to achieve maximum results. You'll learn how to stay creative and focused, work successfully with family and friends, and deal with negatives and distractions. When you master these secrets of success, you will be ready to begin your Six Week Adventure!

Secret 1: Work smarter for greater results

Prepare smarter. When you decide which systems you want to set in motion during your Adventure, start developing them ahead of time. You will work smarter if you hit the ground running.

Plan smarter for greater efficiency. Learn to use information to set up multiple sources for maximum results. If you set up streams that require your direct involvement for just a short time, streams that continue to provide income for a long time, you will have the right strategy. A champion of this approach is Robert Kiyosaki, who suggests that you develop systems that eventually work on their own. These are systems that take care of themselves and do not require your hands-on involvement all the time.

Network Marketing is a good example. If you get in a good position with a Network Marketing enterprise and develop a good down line, you can at some point stop working the system and move on, knowing your income will continue. Book writing is another endeavor that generates long-term income without long-term involvement. You can write a book once and still have copies selling thirty years later.

Look to the Internet for other ideas. Become an infopreneur, a word coined by Robert Allen and others to refer to a person who creates and sells information products. Develop a product or information service that can be delivered electronically. You will receive income for very little work down the road.

The returns on self-perpetuating streams are not instantaneous. But if you put some effort into developing them now, the return will be great in the future. Working smarter requires that you take the long view. Set up a business, work it for a time, create a down line, let it do its own thing and you'll continue to make money over time.

Working smarter also means leveraging. I work with partners on almost every project. Time is precious and it is easier to get something going if more than one person's energy is involved.

You also get into less trouble when you bring more perspectives to a project. I think about the disciples Peter and John. I'm most like Peter. I always get caught with my foot in my mouth. I need a partner like the apostle

John to keep me squared away! One of the biggest advocates of this philosophy is Mark Victor Hansen of ***Chicken Soup for the Soul*** fame. At one of his events I attended, he told us he does almost everything in business with a partner.

When what you do externally is congruent with what's important to you internally you will do it with passion and enthusiasm.
– Brian Tracy

March 14, 2003 – Roger's journal entry

One of the Internet infopreneur streams I have been working is the Seasilver Network Marketing idea. I am not sure I am cut out for this thing, but I spent a good part of the day working on possible strategies to get this thing going. I did this at the computer while working the deal on the house we are seeking to buy.
This evening I went over to a friend's house. He and I are going to do an info-product that we think is going to be a winner. It is so cool to have a friend who is so jazzed about this stuff. I will put more info on our website in the coming weeks on this project.
What a week!

Secret 2: Enthusiasm can make miracles

Enthusiasm is infectious and a powerful tool for change and influence. I also believe it is a soothing and important element for the individual. As we think, so shall we be. If we choose to fail we most likely will, but if we choose to succeed, we have given ourselves a chance to make it. Enthusiasm is the way to accomplish this.

Robert Allen advises that when you launch a new project, your enthusiasm carries through to the people you approach with it. Success is yours! Rabbi Lapin makes the same point. He says the more people you know, the wealthier you'll be. As you learn to network and get to know people, as you start to trust them and vice versa, opportunities will fall into your lap.

Success for an entrepreneur is largely based on reputation and word of mouth. Meet people and capture them with your enthusiasm. Let them see your vision, your passion and desire to make things happen. When you get them excited about working with you, opportunities will open for you. Try it and you will be amazed at the results.

This strategy refers not only to new contacts but also to your family, friends and mentors. There's no better way to find a mentor. No one wants to be around a person whose outlook on life is fatalistic. Mentors don't have time for people who are afraid to take action. One of the reasons I have two mentors in my life is that they both enjoy my enthusiasm.

Secret 3: Concentration and focus can make the difference

Most people have no idea
of the giant capacity
we can immediately command
when we focus all of our resources
on mastering a single area of our lives.
– Anthony Robbins

Concentration and focus are at the root of this Adventure. Concentrating on your financial future, deciding what to do and taking six weeks to change your focus... that's really what the Six Week Adventure is. You won't necessarily achieve spectacular results right away but if you use this time to focus on changing, you will emerge in good shape.

The difficulty when you set aside six weeks to concentrate on a life-changing process is that the simple things of life can get in the way. You might find a new killer series on TV and it might be on at the time you have allotted to spend with your kids. You figure you'll adjust your schedule just this once and it won't hurt. But it might. Practice focusing and put those distractions in their proper place.

If it's a challenge to keep your concentration during your Adventure, the challenge will increase if you have to go back to your regular job at the end of the six weeks. Even though you know you've set good systems in place, systems that might allow you to leave your job and begin a new lifestyle in the very near future, this in-between time can be tough. Yet you need to concentrate on growing these systems. This time to focus is of the greatest importance.

To maintain your concentration and focus during your Adventure and after, remember your enthusiasm. Keep your passion for the project alive and you will stay on track. Beware of potential distractions. Some are unavoidable, but as long as you are aware and do not let them break your concentration for too long, you can maintain your focus. Here are some of the most important areas you need to be aware of:

- **TV can be a distraction**
  It wouldn't hurt to add some TV time to your schedule, just to help you keep the temptation under control. When you sit down and map out your TV time, you will be surprised to discover how much you normally watch!

- **Family, if they are not involved in your Adventure, can be a distraction**
  Balance is important here. You need to schedule time to spend with your family. If you take care of them, you will be able to spend the rest of your time focused on your Adventure. Remember that the Adventure concerns your family whether or not they are involved directly. Part of taking care of your family is concentrating on your income. They need you to be successful!

- **Your job can distract even when you are on leave**
  During our Adventure, the guy who filled in for me kept calling me to ask questions. I finally stopped returning his calls. We needed the time he was taking away from us.

- **Crises are unavoidable**
  They will happen and you need to take care of them. But remember to return your focus to your Adventure when the crisis is over. It's easy to become overwhelmed at the thought of lost time, particularly

when you are on a fixed schedule. Don't lose more time worrying about it. Accept that you lost focus for a while and move on. Concentrate on whatever it takes to get back with the program. You have a choice in life to look backward or forward. Looking back hasn't earned me a single penny or friend. It hasn't done a thing to improve my health. Get up and be positive about the future. Allow the past to have its part in your life but leave it in the past. Move forward.

- **Pets take time to care for**
  Our dog passed away just a few weeks after our Adventure ended. She was sick during the entire six weeks. We spent a lot of time caring for her. Yet we persisted with our Adventure.

- **Watch out for things that can become obsessive.** Beware of becoming bored as well. When you work hard on something for an extended amount of time, you

March 16, 2003
Roger's journal entry

Today I worked on the deal for our first purchase. It looks like the guy will take our offer. Just needs a little tweaking. It is a great house and we have three farming possibilities that should prove quite profitable.

The bigger thing that happened today was my meeting with one of the people I have been seeking a mentoring relationship with. He is from our Bible Study, so we know each other from more than one place.

However, this is the first time I have talked one-on-one with him. I learned a lot from him just in those two hours. I am not sure if he really knows how important this time was for me. I am looking forward to seeking his advice in the coming days, months and years. I went home very excited and worked on Real Estate stuff for the rest of the day.

****

It is the little things you do
that can make a big difference.
What are you attempting to accomplish?
What little thing can you do today
that will make you more effective?
You are probably only one step away from greatness.
-Bob Proctor

start to feel deprived. Burned out. This is very dangerous and is one reason free time is an important part of your Adventure schedule. Allow yourself some down time to relax. When you return to concentrate on setting new systems into place, your work will have your full attention.

March 17, 2003
Roger's journal entry

The offer was accepted and we signed the papers for Escrow! WOW! We got owner financing at 6.5% on 475k of the 535k and I have already made arrangements to refinance 100% of the purchase price once we close on May 1. So it will be 0 down after all is said and done... I will do a detailed accounting of it later. It's too late at night for that right now.

The reason it is so late is that Steve was here and we did the final MP3 version of the interview. He left after 12:30am... and I am going to bed. The audio sounded good. I hope people find it interesting.

You built a plan. You prepared for it. Use your schedule and plan as a guide to avoid these and other pitfalls. Of course this preparation is not a panacea, but it certainly is a good start.

Be in regular touch with your team and give your supportive friends and family permission to ask hard questions during your Adventure. With the right team in place, you'll have the support you need to deal with every distraction. A few good mentors who are really there for you... family and partners who care what's going on... these people will help you stay on track. They'll remind you what you're doing and why. So set up your team early!

One trick I use to stay focused is to turn every challenge into a game. I set up a point system such that when I reach a certain goal, I reward myself. For each action step I complete on time, I award myself a point. I give bonus points for finishing early and subtract points for finishing late. I decide ahead of time what number of points I need to get a particular reward. If I reach x number of points, for example, I will treat myself to a movie.

This type of mental strategy is effective. Try it! It's fun and it helps you stay focused. With focus comes success!

Secret 4: Engage your family and friends with your dreams

You are not here merely to make a living. You are here in order to enable the world to live more amply, with greater vision, with a finer spirit of hope and achievement. You are here to enrich the world, and you impoverish yourself if you forget the errand.
– Woodrow Wilson

I have always been able to turn to my family for moral support in every endeavor. I am fortunate in that respect. If your friends provide more support than your family, you can turn to them. When you engage the people closest to you with your dreams, you create a network of support that will help you stay focused on your Adventure.

Sometimes things will get in the way of your progress. We've discussed some of these already. Who better to keep you going than your family and friends? And what better way for them to help than if they already understand what this Adventure means to you. They might not get the entire Adventure concept or agree with you on everything, but if your Adventure is important to you, it will be important to them that you succeed... and that you enjoy it.

How do you tell your family and friends what you're doing? Be straightforward and explain the Adventure to each family member or friend in whatever way they will best understand. If they are business types, be prepared to discuss your business plan. If their relationship to you is more emotional, share your feelings. Tell them why this Adventure is what you want for your life right now. Just use your best judgment in how to approach them.

Even if you think they'll resist the idea, it's better to be open and share your plans. In some cases the simplified version will do. Tell them you are setting up a new business that will allow you to work independently, that will free you from concerns over job security. Keep it simple but tell them something. Don't think you have to do everything in secret. When you hide things deliberately, you might start to question your own integrity. Because honesty is so important to your success on this Adventure, you want to adhere to that principle in everything you do.

Your family and friends might surprise you and embrace the idea for themselves. Give them opportunities to prosper! Friends and family can be great sources for partnerships and strategic alliances. Sharing your success is a great way to encourage their growth and yours. It is a way to offer your mentorship to them!

Whether or not they want to be involved directly, family and friends can help you network and find valuable resources. We have a terrific bank that provides highly personal service and great value. We found that bank through our parents! Your family or friends might know Stockbrokers, Realtors and business owners who might be interested in working with you. They might refer you to potential business partners or mentors. Word of mouth is a reliable way to find new business resources, and when the reference comes from a trusted friend or family member, you'll feel more confident exploring the new relationship.

Family and friends are also sometimes a good source of capital. If you do allow family or friends to invest in your projects, it is important to treat these as strictly business investments. You are honor-bound to pay back money loaned in good faith. Structure each deal accordingly.

When you first discuss your plans for the Six Week Adventure with family and friends, you can expect one of the following reactions:

- **Enthusiasm:** They might embrace the whole concept and follow alongside. This is what my parents have done. They are working the Real Estate streams with us and assisting on other projects.

- **Caution:** I have a friend who examined the idea of the Six Week Adventure cautiously. After he completed his own research, he started on some Real Estate projects. People who approach the Adventure with caution are the show-me types. They will be honest and fair in their assessments.

- **Indifference:** Some people just won't care one way or the other!

- **Skepticism:** Some of your friends or family might claim to have tried it already. They'll voice skepticism particularly at your first mention of Network Marketing as a possible stream. "I've heard that old Amway spiel one too many times, " they will say. Allow them to have their say then prove them wrong by example. Many people feel trapped in their current situations and wish they could find a way out. They won't move until you prove to them you can do this without failure. Show them!

- **Hostility:** We discuss under "Secret 6" how to deal with naysayers. For now, it's enough to suggest that if someone reacts with hostility, don't discuss your Adventure with them again. You've told them what you're doing and why. Once is enough.

Regardless of how you approach them, how much you tell them or how they react, family and friends can be a great source of support. Don't leave them out. The Six Week Adventure might be just what they are looking for. You never know until you share the idea with them. They'll return the favor by looking out for you.

****

Human beings, by changing the inner attitudes
of their minds, can change the outer aspects
of their lives.
- William James

Secret 5: Allow your life to change

Change is not easy but it is the central focus of the Six Week Adventure. As you embark on this Adventure, you become aware that a new way to live and make money waits for you at the other end. You will change along the way. You have to in order to succeed. Change is part of the process.

Just as importantly, you need to prepare to succeed from the outset. Right now, start by learning how to focus and think outside the box. The preparatory exercises we discussed in Chapter 4 will help you. Understand that through your Adventure, you will change your life. Accept it, prepare for it and your path will be smoother.

Don't be afraid to change. Most people are, and a healthy dose of caution is fine. That's why you're reading this book. You want to know what you're getting into. It's all part of the preparation. But it's vital that you not let your fear of change control you. Learn to make the decisions that will allow you to succeed. Understand that change can be a life enhancer that will let you explore larger possibilities.

If change frightens you considerably, you have all the more reason to address it now before you begin your Adventure. Start by understanding and believing that your Adventure will end in suc-

Learn to Ask!

So, here I am in the middle of our fourth week and we have been through quite a bit! I am sure of one thing: The last three weeks have been worth it! Our lives will never be the same again and that is a very good thing. As I read over last week's newsletter, I realized I could never have said things like that a year ago! Today I am a 100% believer in what this whole adventure is all about. We have had our pitfalls but we have had some great victories.

Now that you have heard my little cheerleading blurb, I want to mention two things here. When we started this project we had certain goals. Marita was going to do her first trade by the end of the six weeks, we were going to purchase at least two houses and we were going to get started on the infopreneur projects.

Marita is paper trading at this point and it is going well. I think that she will be able to make that first real trade in the coming weeks. We have started working with the ghost-writer, and the video project is under way. The big news is that we went

cessful change and that your life will improve as a result. Then move toward those changes one small step at a time. Each time you experience a success, celebrate! Then step up to a new level of change. As you go along, the concept of change will become second nature. By the time your Adventure is over, you will be glad you allowed your life to change!

Secret 6: Deal with the Big Four obstacles

The ultimate measure of a man
is not where he stands
in moments of comfort
and convenience,
but where he stands
at times of challenge
and controversy.
– Martin Luther King, Jr.

Naysaying the naysayers

Some people will express strong opposition to the life change you are trying to make – or the way you approach it. They will criticize and might go so far as to warn you away from this project. They will talk only about what can go wrong. These are the naysayers and no matter how many positive arguments you offer, they will not accept your ideas.

Ideally it's best not to deal with them at all beyond your initial conversation about your Adventure. Naysayers can drain you mentally

to escrow today on the purchase of our first investment property!

It is a biggie too! We purchased it at 535k with great owner financing and very little down. After we do a few more things with the deal, after 90 days, we will get our down payment back as well. Best of all, we will be getting at least 70k in equity! We take possession of the property June 1.

Now our big question is how we are going to farm it. We have several plans on a list ranked from number 1 to number 5. We will simply go down the list until we get it right. One of the options is to move into that house and sell ours. We have a lot of equity in this place as well and it might make more sense for us to sell here rather than there.

One of the biggest bonuses that came with this property is that the seller is a long-time Real Estate investor himself. He is an incredible guy and I think I have found a wonderful mentor for Real Estate investing. As this week progressed, I have spoken to three other people I consider mentors as well. I am discovering that all you have to do is ask.

and leave you discouraged if you let them. Staying on a positive track is difficult enough already! This is your life, your Adventure. Stay on it. If keeping your focus straight ahead means ignoring the naysayers then that's what you have to do.

This doesn't mean that you abandon your relationships with them completely. If they are important people in your life, just deal with them on your usual terms. Find other things to talk about besides your Adventure. If they ask, give a simple answer and move on to a different subject.

And therein lies the lesson for the day! Asking for what you want is probably one of the most important things you can do to succeed as an entrepreneur! As I have been going along on this drastic change in my life, I have realized it is a rough road if you try to go it alone. I am amazed how many people are so willing to help. You will find all kinds of helpful people as well if you take the chance and ask.

The cash conundrum: lack of money or too much of it

Lack of money. A lack of money can make it seem difficult to get your adventure off the ground. Don't let circumstances hold you back. You can find ways to address this obstacle. If you are ready and determined to move ahead, do not let lack of money delay your Adventure.

You can take the free Real Estate course at **johnchilders.com.** This is an honest-to-goodness, meat-on-the-bones Real Estate self study course. It does a great job of talking about nothing-down strategies for Real Estate investment as an income stream. While it is wise to learn from more than one resource, this course is an awesome starting point.

Network Marketing companies have a deserved bad reputation and I must admit they still make me a little squeamish. But they can be moneymakers. The new so-called third wave companies are much more on the up and up and their sales tactics are not as frustrating or pushy. You can get involved with little monetary investment.

In order to succeed with Network Marketing, you need a high level of energy. I recommend you read several books on Network Marketing to get started. A good source of information is Daren Falter at **networkmarketingonthenet.com**.

Ideas are worth money. If you have a great moneymaking idea but no money, you might want to use your Six Week Adventure to draw up a business plan and find investors to buy your idea.

Even better, why not sell half the idea and create a partnership with someone who has the money? Real Estate investors do this all the time. For your share, you can provide the legwork. Say you find a $500, 000 house that, with some cosmetic changes and yard work would sell for $700, 000. You can get an owner-financed deal with $60, 000 down. Are there others out there who would loan you $60, 000 for a year in order to double their money? You bet! They provide the money and you do the cleanup. You both win. Then you come away with the cash to invest in another project.

March 21, 2003
Roger's journal entry

Today is Friday and it was good but not that eventful. Mark Victor Hansen did most of the speaking, later joined by John Childers. It was a good time and I was able to reach my goal of distributing all my CDs and cards. This was big!

There were two other things. First, we got a report from Mark Victor Hansen about Robert Allen's condition. It was a pretty bad accident, but I was encouraged that he seemed to be doing so well.

Lastly, I got together with Dave and his girlfriend, Norma. It was a wonderful meal and I was very encouraged to see how well they are getting along. We took some time and talked about Real Estate and how it can be a financial boom. After they dropped me at the hotel, I realized I had learned a whole lot! Now I can go home and realize that I do know something.

My point is this: if you want to do something badly enough, you will find a way!

If you lack money and none of these suggestions appeals to you, give yourself the luxury to learn, plan and prepare. It might take six months to a year or longer. But when you finally begin your Adventure, you will be ready at a level that you have chosen.

For us, the preparatory work that led up to our Six Week Adventure was as important as the actual Adventure. Establishing a budget, researching the various sources of income, discussing our strengths and weaknesses and evaluating what we could do with the resources we had... our success was as much a function of preparation as anything.

If you decide to wait and build your monetary resources before you embark on your Adventure, take the advice of every millionaire out there and pay yourself first! Learn to budget and allocate your available funds so you have the ability to change your financial fortune. Start putting money aside on a regular basis to finance your Adventure. Otherwise you risk continuing in the same cycle and your Adventure will never get off the ground.

Earlier in the book I suggested breakout for a budget that was adapted from several teachers, most notably T. Harve Eker of Peak Potentials. Let's review it briefly, it is that important! If you can't divide everything this way right now, start working up to it. Good habits start hard, but deliver real benefits once established and regularly practiced!

10%	to your long term investment fund... this is the ground floor of your investing
20%	to save for capital purchases such as a car, major house repair, etc.
50-55%	to expenses
10%	to fun
5- 10%	to giving
10%	to your education – learning is the difference between success and ignorance

Divide it this way and you will succeed. It's that simple. As mentioned before, Eker even suggests you set up jars and divide the funds into the jars labeled appropriately. Then establish separate bank accounts for each division. This is a good idea we are starting to follow. Eker's plan makes saving fun!

Too much money. Here's a problem you might not expect to be a problem: too much money! Believe it or not, too much money at the start can make your Adventure as difficult as a lack of funds. If you have more than enough money to float you on this Adventure, beware of the three deadly C's:

- **Creativity loss:** Money can buy a lot of things. When you set up your multiple sources, money becomes a bad substitute for creativity. Rather than think of options that are effective and exciting, you might be tempted down one of the avenues that simply requires money. This might not be the best way and if you don't do your research, you'll miss that. Lack of money forces you to do careful research and think of alternatives. The wealthiest people I know are ingenious when it comes to creativity. They learn not to use their money as a crutch. They learn to create ideas and then use their resources to bring their visions to reality.

- **Carelessness:** There are so many ways to make money out there that you can easily try to buy anything that looks good. We made this mistake when we purchased a mortgage-buying package. It was not right for us. We bought it without thinking through what we really wanted and needed. You need time to check things out and to see how your situation develops. Easy access to money can lead you to hasty decisions and purchases, and in the end your money will be wasted. Things to look out for are print resources, software packages, workshops and organizational memberships among others. All of these are great resources and if you need something, that's fine. Just be sure you think it through first and be sure it's really what you need.

****

It's always fun to do the impossible.
- Walt Disney

- **Complacency:** Simply put, too much money can make you lazy. Six weeks can turn into a nice long vacation rather than a time of concentration and focus on life change. It is an easy time to fritter away a lot of money. This is one reason we can't encourage you enough to start your Adventure with a solid plan!

Probably the best way to combat the problem of too much money is to create a budget, as we suggested earlier, and give yourself an allowance. Create the discipline to avoid these deadly three C's and you will put yourself miles ahead.

Personal difficulties

Life does not stop or go on hold for your Adventure. You will experience personal distractions. The kids might get sick, your mother might fall down and bruise her hip or your pet may die. Your seasonal hay fever might kick in. Your car might fall apart on you. As we all know, the list of life's distractions can be endless.

The Six Week Adventure is designed for the real world. You may take time off from work to set new systems into place, but you can't take time off from your life. The Adventure requires you to do the work in the everyday world.

The biggest difficulties we experienced during our Adventure were of a personal nature and involved a certain amount of hurt. Sometimes we had to take a day off from our Adventure, as we would from any normal job. The next day, although the hurt was not gone, we did get back to our projects.

We also went through difficulties with our dog. She was old and grew steadily weaker during our six weeks. We lost her a few weeks after our Adventure ended. A pet, even one that is sick, is relatively easy to care for, so she did not distract us with a lot of extra work. But her worsening condition was a constant emotional drain.

As we mentioned earlier when we talked about the

need to stay focused, your spouse, family and friends are there to support you and to help you keep perspective. Guard these relationships and you will get through your Adventure regardless of the personal distractions.

There is no magical way to keep personal distractions from occurring or to put them on the back burner. Just be responsible. Stay focused when it comes to your business. But remember why we strongly recommend you compartmentalize your time. You still have a personal life to lead!

March 22, 2003
Marita's journal entry

I spent the day with my friend Mary. We went to the Northwest Women's Show. It was a huge event in which you could get information about everything make-up to home repair. I even got to see Richard Simmons close up. The interesting thing that happened was that I got out of my comfort zone. Instead of just picking up information or listening to an answer to a question asked by others, I asked questions to seek specific knowledge on things related to self-employment. It was an exciting time. I guess I need to get out of my box more often.

External distractions and world events

During our six weeks, war started in Iraq. I personally know a number of people who were very distracted and preoccupied by the whole thing. One of my friends calculated that he spent 40-50 hours a week watching the entire war on FOX News. World events will affect you. War, terrorism, the Stock Market, your favorite football team losing, or a rainout at the World Series are all distractions that might cause you to lose focus. Something is always happening and always will be. Don't allow yourself to become distracted. Short of war coming to your door, put things into perspective and stay the course.

Whereas I am a bit of a risk taker, I am married to a woman for whom stability is very important. We are trying to find a safe platform from which I can leap occasionally without causing her excessive stress. Therefore I do give thought to putting systems into place that will allow us to grow without causing too much uncertainty. I want to create an income strategy that will create greater stability and security for us.

The Six Week Adventure is by its very nature a potential risk. Uncertainty waits at the other end. But is your current situation secure? No! A corporate job and a steady paycheck might offer the illusion of security, but look around. Layoffs abound. No one is secure. The instability of the world motivates me to press forward toward a better and more prosperous future.

We face risk in everything we do. We drive from point A to point B every day and seldom think about the hundreds of people that die in automobile accidents on a daily basis. We eat food purchased at a grocery store and trust it will not make us sick. Why? Because we know precautions are taken that make these activities – and hundreds like them – relatively safe and worth taking on the challenge.

Secret 7: Learn what it takes to get there

> *Opportunity is missed by most people because it is dressed in overalls and looks like work.*
> - Thomas A. Edison

To be successful, you need to spend the time and learn what it takes to get there. Learn from everything. Apply what is worth applying and discard what does not work. Successful people do these things as a matter of habit.

I love sports. I enjoy watching college football and major league baseball in particular. So much that I would listen to our local sports radio station all the time in my car. One day, I added up all the time I spent listening and discovered it equaled between 8-12 hours a week! All for only 15 to 20 minutes of information that was better obtained from a newspaper.

So I decided to use that commute time to listen to instructional tapes and CDs that would help me prepare for my future business ventures. Do you realize that amount of time is the length of the average home study course each week? It took me about a week to get into it. Now I listen to the news and one sports report every morning and evening and then I move on to the educational tapes. Not only am I learning more. I am now a better driver who is less prone to get upset!

Learn to change your habits. Learn to develop the ones that will help you win. Make the extraordinary effort to learn what it takes to do what you want. This is the theme of this whole book! It is a significant key to your success on this Adventure.

We want you to succeed and we know the journey has its challenges. We hope we have given you the information you need to maximize your experience and deal with the challenges in the most effective ways possible.

****

Life is a series of experiences,
each one of which makes us bigger...
For the world was built to develop character,
and we must learn
that the setbacks and grief we endure
help us in our marching onward.

-Henry Ford

PART III

YOUR TIME HAS COME!
Let's do your Adventure

It's a job that's never started
that takes the longest to finish.
- J. R. R. Tolkien

CHAPTER 8

THE FIRST FEW DAYS: Set up your Adventure

The act of taking the first step
is what separates the winners from the losers.
- Brian Tracy

Set up your dreaming session – a short retreat

You've done the preparation and drawn up your plans. You are ready to start your Six Week Adventure. Kick off your Adventure with a short retreat before you start on the work full force. A retreat will give you the chance to go over your plans, to take a big breath so you can hit the ground running. And a chance to celebrate that you made it to the starting gate!

I am a strong believer in marking passages in life with a celebration. This is a big undertaking. You are about to spend six weeks, at the end of which your life will be changed forever. It took courage to get to this point. Go ahead and celebrate!

We took a short retreat at the start of our Adventure to celebrate, to warm up and to start our journal and get our newsletter going. The retreat is not a delay. It is an important way to begin your Adventure. When you go on your retreat, you are no longer in the planning stage. Your Adventure has started!

We used a trip to Orlando for a Robert Allen Millionaire retreat as our opportunity for this part of our Adventure. We took the whole first week of our Adventure because it overlapped with the Orlando retreat. I recommend that you start your retreat on the Friday leading into your six weeks. Take the entire weekend and go to your favorite getaway. Use this time to get your mind focused completely on your plans and to take a breather before your Adventure work begins full time.

March 23, 2003
Roger's journal entry

Today was all about talking with people. Most notable was my conversation with my folks. They seem to be picking up on the wealth mentality I have been talking about with them. Dad is doing the Tax Lien certificates for us. He is now interested in helping me with some of the other ventures. We are going to do some more great things together.

During our kickoff retreat, the first thing we did each morning was to discuss our three initial projects. Then we wrote our journal entries and conducted what business we could from our hotel. We spent the rest of the day enjoying the attractions.

During the day and in the evenings we talked about what the future would be like. This is one reason your retreat time is so important. When you start on a journey, you need to know where you are headed. Envisioning the future is important to this type of undertaking. You need to remember a simple principle: you are what you think about. Earl Nightingale was the big advocate for this small but powerful truth – check out his book ***The Strangest Secret*** if you can find it. Part of becoming is choosing your path. Remember your goals and make real those things you strive for.

Our discussions covered a lot of territory and unfortunately we didn't approach this time in an organized fashion. A lot of what we discussed we didn't write down. I would encourage you to approach your retreat with better planning than we did. Create a dream book. You can incorporate this into your journal if you'd like. Write want for your future – a descriptions and save pictures of what you more elaborate version of the sketch you did during your planning sessions. Reaffirm your goals for the coming Adventure. Do the work in the morning and evening. The rest of the time, enjoy yourself!

Take the time during your retreat to write down your first three project goals. Ours were to (1) buy an investment home, (2) set up a broker account and make our first trade by the end of the six weeks, and (3) establish our website and start our newsletter. After you list your first project goals, read over your list every day and then do the work.

The retreat is also the time to establish your daily routine for the six weeks. It's important that you sketch out your routine in detail then stick to it. The more we kept to our plan, the better things went. Set a priority list that will allow you to structure your day so that your most important tasks come first. If diet change is important, consider documenting and envisioning those goals as well.

We felt a great deal of apprehension before getting started. Our kickoff retreat allowed us to sharpen our focus on the tasks ahead. Despite our research and planning, the retreat was the first chance we had to leave everything else behind – like my job – and switch our mental gears completely toward our Adventure. It marked a clear transition where the past ended and the future began. Our kickoff date is an anniversary we will celebrate every year.

****

Life affords no higher pleasure
than that of surmounting difficulties,
passing from one step of success to another,
forming new wishes and seeing them gratified.
- Samual Johnson

Create your personal routine

Our daily routine turned out to be really important in terms of structuring our time, helping us keep our focus and moving us steadily toward our goals. I recommend the following guidelines when you create your six-week schedule:

- **Design a daily routine**
- **Stick to your schedule but don't allow it to rule you**
- **Write it down**
  Putting your schedule in writing not only helps you stick to it but also helps you keep your activities in perspective, so they don't seem overwhelming. A written schedule gives you a yardstick by which to measure your accomplishments. We posted some of our tasks on our bathroom mirrors! The refrigerator is another good place to put these reminders.
- **Do not neglect your personal time**
  Include it in your schedule.
- **Remember to schedule time for learning**
  Learning is a critical part of the Adventure. The central purpose of the Six Week Adventure is to change your life. Learning is one of the keys to successful change. Don't just plan a generic daily routine for the six weeks. Keep a calendar for each day and fill it in according to your schedule and the specific projects you will pursue. Here are some helpful hints:
- **Establish your business day**
  We used 7am to 5pm every day.
- **At the beginning of each business day, make two lists that contain the tasks for the day**
  One in order of importance and the other in an order that reflects the tasks you like to do most. Start with the most important item then move to the most enjoyable task. Alternate back and forth throughout the day. Eventually your two lists will start to resemble each other, but I recommend keeping the two lists

separate for quite awhile. Rewarding yourself after a tough task by switching to something you love will add spice to your day.

- **At the close of each business day write down all of your accomplishments**
  Also write down everything you need to work on the next day.

- **Remain flexible**
  Life does not always fit into a schedule. Use the schedule as a guide and as a task bar to hold you to your daily goals, but you might need to adjust it according to your immediate needs. When you stray, use the schedule to get back on track.

We weren't always able to stick to our schedule. Especially with Real Estate, time must be flexible. But we tried to complete all of our daily tasks as close to schedule as possible.

Review your schedule daily and make adjustments as necessary. Remember the purpose of the schedule is to help you stay on track and meet your goals. As your projects evolve and your goals start to crystallize, you will need to make modifications. We reviewed and updated our schedule every day. As to the overall routine, you will want to review that weekly to be sure it fits the style of work that your chosen income streams demand. Above all else, your schedule must help you work productively.

As we mentioned in our discussion about preparation, you can start to phase in your daily schedule before you begin your Adventure. Some tasks you can start beforehand as well. I started making Real Estate calls a month before our Adventure began. Other things that you can start in advance include paper trading and article writing. The most effective way to phase in your new routine is to maintain some amount of consistency while introducing flexibility and new tasks.

The most difficult aspects of creating your personal routine will be sticking to a regular schedule, making time for yourself and not overworking. In the beginning you might be tempted to work too hard on your Adventure, because you are eager to get started and overwhelmed with the amount of work that lies ahead of you. Resist this tendency and be disciplined in allocating time for yourself. This will become even more critical as the six weeks progress, so get into the habit from the beginning.

Remember, the Six Week Adventure is designed to help you focus on new ways to earn an income. This is part of an overall lifestyle change that will lead to more freedom and control, more time for your family and yourself. Your new income streams are one part of a well-rounded life. The changes you set into place during your Adventure need to benefit you in every facet of your life.

March 24, 2003 – Marita's journal entry

I met with my friend Jane today for a walk and coffee. It was such a beautiful sunny day. We walked, talked and rested on benches in the sun. It was so peaceful. We talked about her retirement from teaching and my year off. She was a great help because I am wondering: Do I look for a teaching job for the next school year?

Her wisdom came through as she asked about my grieving for my mom. Both of her parents died closely together too and she was as close to her parents as I was to mine. She can totally relate. It became clear that I'm not ready to go back into teaching and that I need to grieve more. So we cried and laughed together about the pits of being orphans. It is so heart breaking at times and I miss my folks so much.

Establish your Adventure schedule

Part of creating your daily routine is figuring out what part of each day or which days of the week you will devote to a particular stream. It's important to map out whatever you can in advance, although it's difficult: you don't necessarily know up front everything you will be doing during the six weeks. Opportunities will arise and new developments will take place that will shape your schedule. One deal might lead to another unexpected deal and your schedule will need to be adjusted.

It's best to start out with a concrete plan as you envision the six weeks unfolding. Then when things change, be prepared to accommodate those changes without losing track of the plans you've already set in motion.

Most likely, for every new task you have to fit into your schedule you'll find another that takes less time than you'd allotted. Things tend to work out that way if you're organized going in.

We developed a preliminary schedule and stuck to it as much as we could. What helped is that we focused on enough streams to make our time effective but not so many that we couldn't handle them all. So our schedules were full but manageable. Marita did the paper trading and then went about doing her housework. I did Real Estate on Monday and Thursday almost exclusively and then worked Internet projects through the rest of the week.

This is how my original weekly schedule looked:

MONDAY

- Plan the day
- Make Real Estate calls
- Visit local Real Estate possibilities
- Work on offers for Real Estate
- Write journal entry

TUESDAY

- Plan the day
- Make Real Estate calls
- Work on Seasilver business on the web
- Research new web-based avenues for Seasilver
- Write journal entry

WEDNESDAY

- Plan the day
- Make Real Estate calls
- Update main website
- Write journal entry

THURSDAY

- Plan the day
- Visit Olympia, Washington Real Estate possibilities
- Work on offers for Real Estate
- Write journal entry

FRIDAY

- Plan the day
- Make Real Estate calls
- Schedule lunch with someone to network with
- Work on offers for Real Estate
- Write journal entry

SATURDAY

- Spend morning on learning activities related to my chosen income streams

SUNDAY

- In the evening, prepare for the next day

Notice three things from the above schedule:

(1) you are spending full time on this Adventure;

(2) you need to schedule some time for networking and learning;

(3) you need to schedule time for family and for yourself.

Does your schedule stay fixed throughout your Adventure? Not necessarily. It's important to plan but also to be flexible to accommodate the needs that arise as a result of your Adventure.

I am a planner by trade and the biggest lesson I have learned is not to over-plan. The schedule above is at about the right level for initial planning. I think that getting to this level is helpful but we didn't always follow it exactly. Life sometimes got in the way and our Adventure sometimes generated new opportunities – and obstacles – that were cause for adjustment.

For example, we found our first house very quickly, so most of the six weeks was spent negotiating and closing the deal rather than doing the research mapped out in the above schedule. Had we not found that opportunity right away, my schedule would have continued to look more like the original. Of course, I did devote time to research in pursuit of our next property. The Seasilver project also took much less time than anticipated, so I used the time freed up by that project to start work on this book sooner than expected.

While we kept our schedules flexible and adjusted them as we moved along, the most important step was to plan each day before it happened. Even if that meant mapping out the following day the night before. It's important going into each new day to have a sense of what is going to happen. That information will help you keep your Adventure on target.

Set aside five to ten percent of your time to give away

This is an important block of time to work into your schedule. We are part of a society that has many needs. I always wonder if I am part of the problem or part of the solution. One of the objectives of the Six Week Adventure is to become accustomed to being part of the solution.

There are 168 hours in a seven-day week and the average person sleeps seven to nine hours. Assuming you sleep eight hours per day, multiply that by seven days. That's 56 sleeping hours per week, which means 112 waking hours. You should donate
five to ten percent of those waking hours: roughly 5-11 hours per week.

Giving time to causes you sup-

March 24, 2003
Roger's journal entry

Today marks the real start of the final third of our adventure. Things are looking good and we are making some excellent progress on our adventure. Here is a brief synopsis of what we have been able to accomplish:

Real Estate: We purchased our first property, a wonderful house that is worth in the area of $600, 000. We are very excited to follow through with our farming of this wonderful property. We have a list of four possibilities we will use to turn this into a very profitable situation.

For those naysayers out there, this is an owner-financed deal with a very low down payment. By the time the financing is done it will be a nothing down deal! I am looking forward to completing the deal to a point where I can document it for you in detail. This is really fun stuff.

While we are still looking for that second property to fill our quota for two properties by the end of the adventure, we have exceeded our dollar amount goal! This is very cool! We just need to get that next property to get

port can be a great substitute for giving money. In fact, in some ways this seems a better way to go. It is a great way to keep things in perspective. While one of the goals of this Adventure is to give you the financial freedom to support those causes, giving of your time now will help you realize down the road that time might in some cases be more valuable to your recipients than money.

This five to ten percent of your time is not just for charitable work. Time for your family also needs to be included in the time you give away. Giving away your time simply means taking time you would have spent on your Adventure and giving it to someone else.

If you do 50 hours of Adventure-related work per week and give away another five, you still have 40 hours during the week to take care of other responsibilities included household duties. You can also fit in more time with your family by involving children who are old enough to be part of your Adventure. Just make one of your Adventure goals to teach good financial management to your children!

We spent our give-away time working with our church in Sunday school and on other projects.

Most notably we both took part in cooking for various ministries at

over the hump.

Stocks: Marita is doing very well with her paper trading. I know she feels that she needs more work on it, but I also think she understands much more than she is letting on. At any rate, I think she will be able to make her first trade soon and we will see if this stream is for us.

Information Marketing and Internet: As you can see by our website and this journal, we are amassing a great deal of valuable information for our book. We have hired a ghostwriter. At this time we are working on an outline. It looks as if we will have enough material for the Book Expo in May.

I am working on helping my friend and new partner on a site called www.werecordit.com.
The idea is that we will be supplying recording services for self-published authors and others who want to use audio to supplement their info-products. He is a very talented guy. You will be thrilled if you need his services! I am really excited to see what he can do with this service!

Other Things: A few items don't fit anywhere. I have my own first student

the church as well as supporting various outreach opportunities. We were also involved in working with an adoption agency for a short time.

One of the universal themes I have encountered in virtually every time management course I have ever taken is that we make time for those things that are important to us. Anyone who embarks on the Six Week Adventure will agree that it's important to make the world a better place. You'll be surprised how much good you can do in just five hours a week. It's not much time to give away but the payoff is huge.

If you are taking six weeks away from your job to do this Adventure, you will have more time than you ever thought possible. Give some of it away. It is worth it and you will be the better for it.

Finalize your plans

As you've figured out by now, I believe planning is important. We did some advance preparation for our Adventure but most of it came together very quickly as the start dates approached. It's amazing what you can do when you have a deadline on the horizon!

After years in the planning and project management world, I have come to believe that 98 percent of the human race pro-

in my friend Steve. This is a good thing for me, as I do need to be able to share with him clearly and precisely what he is asking me to share with him. As we develop our info projects, this will be a very valuable experience.

I will also be attending John Childers's speaker training. I am really looking forward to getting down to Las Vegas and learning how to do the speaking that leads to the big bucks. It should be a great time and I am looking forward to the challenge.

We have partnered with my dad to do Tax Lien certificates. We have had a great start but we are looking to do much more! It is an exciting project and we are really looking forward to developing a full-blown strategy that will lead to some very good returns on our money.

Has it been worth it to this point? Yes!!! If everything we have put into place at this time comes together, we will easily make our goal of our first $1 million in net worth. More exciting: at that point I will be able to move on from my regular job. Life is good now and we are going to make it!

crastinates! A date is very important. If you don't have a date forced upon you, set one and work toward it. You might need to scramble to get things done as your date approaches, but working out of the chaos will simply become a part of your Adventure!

Most large corporations have a 60-day layoff notice, so as part of our simulation of a layoff, we started to prepare for our Adventure about two months in advance. We set the date according to factors that came from my work situation. I tried to minimize the impact of my absence. If you are considering a leave of absence as I did, you need to take into account how long it will take to get everything in order. Use your lead-time wisely. If you have to wait four months before you can go on leave, you have two more months of preparation time for your Adventure.

We used a lot of the prep time to research, read and practice. I recommend this strongly. Forearmed is forewarned. It is even okay to start developing one of the streams ahead of time if that will help with your Adventure. For example, I started to call prospective FSBOs – homes For Sale By Owner – two months before our Adventure started. The nature of your Adventure should be your guide. Ultimately your Adventure will be your own creation!

Did I Mention That It is Important to Ask?

OK, I am now a believer. I have listened to a number of tapes. I have heard speaker after speaker. Now I have listened to all but the first CD from Mark Victor Hansen's and Jack Canfield's ***The Aladdin Factor***! I am now convinced that all I need is to ask to get what I want! I mean it. All I have to do is ask. All you have to do is ask.

Sounds so simple, doesn't it, but is it really? Think about it. If it's so easy then why is it so hard? I believe there are four reasons that make it hard for the vast majority of us.

Reason #1: At some point during our lives, we were taught that asking was a sign we were dumb. I can remember many times when I was a little boy listening to others ask questions and get nailed big time for their trouble. As a result, I resolved that the risk was just not worth it. So I learned never to ask. This is an issue for a lot of people. I have had to force myself to resist this fear and the results are amazing. Folks, take the chance and ask the question!

Reason #2: We see ourselves as having a particular station in life. As a result, we don't ask for the better things in life. Many of us were raised by our parents to go to school, get good grades, get a good job, work at that job for 30+ years and then move on to retirement. Along that road, it occurs to precious few of us to ask if there is anything else out there. We just don't ask for the things we yearn for, to seek better things for ourselves, our loved ones and our friends! Nor do we always ask if we can contribute more constructively to bettering the human condition. In effect, we have created our very own version of a cast system. Dare to ask for more and do it regularly. If you do it often, you will be amazed at what can happen!

Reason #3: We hate the word "no." It is hard for any person to take no for an answer. For some reason, we perceive this word as a rejection rather than a simple refusal of a request. When I receive a "no" from someone, I feel that I have somehow offended that person. Sounds kind of crazy but I bet I am not alone! It is important to keep perspective on things. "No" is 99, 999, 999 out of 100, 000, 000 times just a simple reply. No anger or emotional baggage attached! As my friends say to me, so I say to you: Get over it. Realize that "no" is just a pathway to "yes."

Reason #4: We don't believe. While this is not a religious newsletter, I know that most of you by now realize that Marita and I do have a strong belief in God. But belief doesn't always make a difference. Most people who have a belief system don't believe God answers. Sure, we say we do, but the evidence says no. How can a person receive a blessing if s/he doesn't believe that the blesser will do it... or can do it? Can it be so hard for us to realize that if we do believe, that God does want to bless us? Is it so hard to imagine that as a result of God's blessing, we might be allowed to bring blessings to others? For those of

The great French Marshall Lyautey once asked his gardener to plant a tree. The gardener objected that the tree was slow growing and would not reach maturity for 100 years. The Marshall replied, 'In that case, there is no time to lose; plant it this afternoon!'
- John F. Kennedy

He who knows others is wise;
He who knows himself is enlightened.
- Lao-tzu, The Way of Lao-tzu

Take a chance!
All life is a chance.
The man who goes furthest
is generally the one who is willing
to do and dare.
- Dale Carnegie

CHAPTER 9
THE FIRST TWO WEEKS
Establish Your Success Routine

A person's lifestyle is directly related to his/her commitment to excellence.
- Brian Tracy

Implement and follow your schedule

Pick up one of the hundreds of time management books out there and you'll see one point repeated throughout: Stick to your schedule! The more you do this, the more successful you will be.

What these books don't always tell you, though, is that you are human, life is filled with distractions, and projects evolve as they go along. Learn to stick to your schedule but also remember to adapt and update your schedule as things change. After all, the Six Week Adventure is about change!

I originally intended to allot parts of each day to my two streams and provide some support to Marita in her Stock trading. But it turned out my schedule didn't work well that way. Though the time allocated to each stream was the same according to the schedule, in practice it became obvious that each day would have an emphasis on a particular stream.

On Thursdays I ended up working exclusively on Real Estate in Olympia, Washington. It was much easier and made more sense for me to go there and do all the work during a single day. I also had to put a lot more concerted effort into the Real Estate transaction we happened across early in our Adventure. I had to adjust the rest of my schedule to accommodate this unexpected development.

Don't be discouraged during the early days of schedule adjustment: the time when your initial energy has calmed but the schedule hasn't yet become habit. It takes approximately 30 days for a habit to ingrain itself. This is just one more reason it's important to allow six weeks for your Adventure, so that you have plenty of time to form new habits. After your schedule becomes a habit, sticking to it will be easy.

It's a habit well worth developing early on, which is another reason you need to approach the Adventure with the understanding that you will stick to your schedule as closely as possible. Revising your schedule to keep up with new developments in your Adventure is fine: you're still sticking to a schedule, albeit a slightly modified one. But don't stray from the idea of a schedule.

If you have never worked from home before, you'll discover that your schedule is your best defense against distractions. The smallest thing can turn into a multi-hour loss of time. Learning to follow your schedule – even if you had to revise today's schedule last night – can be one of the most effective tools out there to help create an effective and exciting Adventure!

Sticking to my schedule gave me confidence. The idea of working from home was one of my biggest fears. I was not confident I could work from home given all the possible distractions. As our Adventure progressed, I realized I could work from home and be effective. I also learned that a well-organized schedule allowed me to be more productive than I had imagined. Having a schedule and a set of priorities empowered me to focus more easily and avoid the distractions I most feared.

Follow your personal routine

My routine started to feel natural about two weeks into our Adventure. It became even more comfortable by the fourth week. I know sticking to the schedule helped make this routine feel like habit.

The new routine also reinforced right away that we were making a life change. One of the real benefits was the feeling that we were in control of our own destiny. Having a routine that was mine for my business was a wonderful and powerful change in our lifestyle. Our routine helped us achieve success on our Adventure. When you start to put new systems into place, it's important to keep on top of everything you are doing. Without a carefully developed personal routine to follow, you will not be as productive in your Adventure as you could be.

I am not a person of routine, by nature, so this was a new type of practice for me. I liked it a lot and have used some of the tricks I learned in my post-Adventure world.

Here's some of what I learned that I still apply:

- **Eating breakfast.** For years I traded breakfast for an extra 20 minutes of sleep. That has changed. Breakfast is an amazing energy enhancer!

- **Starting the day by reviewing my schedule and prioritizing the day's activities.** This is a wonderful way to get a preview of what the day holds. For me this was very exciting.

- **Making business calls first thing in the day.** This is easy to do and provides a great sense of accomplishment. It also gets out of the way something that could be distracting when I'm concentrating on a project later on.

- **Finishing the day by creating a list for the next morning's work.**

- **Sharing with my wife what is happening.** Sharing the excitement is a wonderful way of keeping the life in the project.

- **Writing down new ideas and goals.** This is one of the practices I built into my Adventure routine. Creativity is important. While it is important to keep a sharp focus, it is also important to be aware of what is coming down the road and to keep looking for new possibilities – opportunities that have just opened up as well as new projects the Adventure has made possible.

March 29, 2003
Roger's journal entry

Ahh… Saturday. Today, I promised Marita and myself that I would take some time away from the six-week effort and do something different. I don't know if I have ever mentioned it, but one of my charities involves making something for a local auction every year. This year, a friend and I are making a children's cradle. It is a great project and I have really been looking forward to working on it. Eight hours today in my shop was so nice. It was a fantastic way to rest and get my mind off everything else.

Deal with the unexpected

Even though you create the time and space necessary to focus on your Adventure, life doesn't stop for you. Not only will you need to deal with personal difficulties and distractions such as we've described in earlier chapters. You will need to be prepared for problems that arise related specifically to your Adventure.

You won't be able to predict everything that might happen, but it's not a bad idea to brainstorm a little and

****

Small opportunities
are often the beginning of great enterprises.
- Demosthenes

think of problems that might arise. We did some brainstorming for our income streams of Real Estate, the Stock Market and the Network Marketing product. Here are some of the potential problems we came up with:

- Our Mortgage Broker or other key person could go on vacation
- A Real Estate seller might have an unusual requirement for the sale
- Our Real Estate exit strategies might fall through
- Car trouble might make it difficult for us to visit Real Estate properties
- Our offer might be accepted too quickly on a Real Estate deal
- Our credit rating might go down because the broker checked our credit too many times
- The Network Marketing venture we work with might encounter legal or supply problems
- We might experience Internet connection failures
- The Stock Market could go through very unpredictable streaks that might require us to sit out
- Our partners might back out
- We might discover our chosen streams are not right for us

As it turns out, we did experience several of these problems. We ran into a Real Estate seller that had unusual requirements and accepted our offer right away on a Real Estate deal. Real Estate is a funny business. The more I delve into it, the more I realize how much I need to learn. The house we bought was on the market a long time, though they had received a number of offers. They wanted the "right people" to buy the house. When we fulfilled that requirement, they accepted our offer quickly with no negotiating. That was a bit disconcerting. I was expecting to have to negotiate. That makes me think I should have offered less.

While it didn't happen during our Adventure, our Network Marketing company was taken to task for exaggerating on their advertising. When we first looked into the deal, they checked out okay. After their advertising tactics came to our attention, we thought long and hard about whether or not we would stay with them. We chose not to. Ethics are important. What this company did reflected badly on us, so we discontinued the relationship. Check everything you do against your ethical standards and make changes, if necessary, along the way.

Brainstorming in advance can really help you prepare for the unexpected. As you prepare your list of potential problems, don't think of them in negative terms. None of these problems might occur. This exercise is simply meant to remind you that the unexpected does happen and that you need to be prepared to deal with it. It might be helpful to look over your list of potential problems and ask yourself how you would get through them. I believe good can come from every situation, so prepare to take a positive approach when difficulties arise.

Do your week ending work

Friday nights were a time when we collapsed a bit and enjoyed each other's company. We talked over much of what we did during

March 30, 2003
Roger's journal entry

This is the first day of the last week of our adventure! Man, has this been an exciting time for us! We have bought a house. We have purchased Tax Lien certificates. I have my first "student" in my friend Steve. By the way, this guy is going to be a real go-getter! The book is being worked. The Seasilver business is going well and my mother is going to get involved in it since my other partnership has gone dormant for the time being. So all is well!

Now all I have to do is get the cash flow up so I can get the whole thing going and get myself out of Boeing. I just like working for myself. It is much more lucrative!

So, for the balance of the day, I did research and paperwork. Oh, yeah, my parents came over. My dad is partnering with us on the Tax Liens and now he is going to work the rental stuff with us as well. It is very exciting and I am ready to get going on this partnership. You see, my dad is one of my best friends and I have always wanted to partner in a business with him. I really hope this works out!

the week. These sessions were an important part of our Adventure. You don't have to pick Friday night, but take some time at the end of each week to do the following:

- **Review your goals:** While it's good to review your goals on a daily basis, be sure to read through your list of Adventure goals at the end of each week. If your spouse is joining you on this Adventure, discuss your goals together. This will help keep your Adventure on track.

- **Review your successes:** It is important to get a clear sense of what you have accomplished during the week.

- **Establish your plan for the next week:** To make my Sunday night/Monday morning planning easier, I took some time Friday night to write down objectives and tasks for the following week. I also took this time to consider whether I might need to modify the weekly schedule I laid out at the beginning of our Adventure.

- **Update your accounting books:** Bookkeeping is not a sexy subject and you might dread it. But it's an important part of the Adventure. You need to track all your expenditures and income and keep your books up to date. The end of the week is a good time to do this. A program like QuickBooks can simplify the process. Set aside time for accounting at the end of every week and soon it will become a habit.

- **Review your cumulative progress:** Though your progress might be based on intangibles at first, continue to measure your achievements in terms of your Adventure goals. What you see will vary depending on the streams you follow and how far into the Adventure you are. But it's still important to track developments in terms of your overall plan. While we didn't expect dynamic results at first, we did expect to see the puzzle come together. And it did!

The end of the week is also a good time to remember that serendipity plays a major role in the success of this Adventure. We started to make money right away from our Network Marketing product and we were fortunate to close a big Real Estate deal. I have become a big believer in the idea that we should expect good things to happen to us. If you take that positive approach to your Adventure and take time at the end of each week to reflect on positive developments, you will succeed.

CHAPTER 10
THE REST OF THE ADVENTURE
Living Your Dream

Everybody builds a dream in their lifetime.
You're either going to build your dream, or somebody else's.
So build your own!
- Christopher LaBrec

Your time is now yours

Your pre-Adventure time is about dreaming, planning and preparing. Your first two weeks are about putting systems into place and learning a new routine. By the third week, your Adventure will be well underway and things will start to feel natural. This is the time to allow flexibility into your schedule and routine. This is the time to start living your dream.

The sooner you recognize that this time is yours – to learn, to grow, to set up new ventures, to live your dream – the more successful your Adventure will be. This is the time for you to explore new possibilities in your income streams, to take advantage of learning opportunities, to network, to expand your horizons, to partner and to move into new areas. Keep your Adventure on track but allow yourself the flexibility to recognize and respond to new opportunities. Make the most of this wonderful gift of time you've given yourself.

As you move further into your Adventure, you will need to focus on what comes next. Your systems are in place now. You are working them and pursuing your strategies to their fullest. Now you need to spend time looking to the future and coming up with answers to these three questions:

- What will you do during the months that follow your Adventure?
- What new opportunities lie in the future?
- What types of learning do you need in order to expand?

By this stage in your Adventure, you should be interacting with mentors and others in a position to help you answer these questions. This might be a good time to establish a policy of meeting new people every week. Go to the Rotary Club or Chamber of Commerce and start getting to know the movers and shakers. These venues are fertile ground for finding partners for future ventures. Partnerships can help you prepare for reentry into your job if you plan to return, and they can help if your funds are short.

When you think about new opportunities to pursue after your Adventure, think about what you love doing. I love the written word and I wanted to share our experiences in the hope we could help others find financial freedom. So I knew this book would be an opportunity to pursue after the six weeks ended. I also discovered how much I love Real Estate. I might consider getting a Realtor's license.

Through your work during the six weeks, you will realize what you still need to learn. This will help you decide what future educational opportunities to pursue. We are doing home study courses at a rate of one or two a month. We read constantly. We attend seminars and workshops periodically. My desire is to attend at least four per year. I cannot emphasize enough how important specialized knowledge is to your success. Get it wherever it is available.

You will have to deal with distractions

As your Adventure moves forward and you get more deeply into working your streams, you will still need to deal with distractions. As we discussed in earlier chapters, we experienced our share of distractions, from a severe setback in our adoption proceedings to the bad health of our dog. Through our experience, we developed some coping strategies:

- **Traumatic distractions:** These are almost a complete surprise and need to be dealt with according to their impact. Be aware that you are human and that some things are more important than work. If it is necessary for you to regain your balance and move forward, take a day or two off. You do this regularly in your work setting. You take a mental health day. You use sick leave to take your son in for an appendectomy. You take time out to attend a funeral. These days off are just as critical when you are self-employed. Don't be afraid to use them. Do stay in touch with your spouse and/or family on these issues. They will know when you are headed in the wrong direction!

- **Family/friend distractions:** If a friend or family member is distracting you, have the fortitude to ask them to understand that you are not on vacation and that you need to focus on your tasks at hand. You might want to explain this to them over a cup of coffee at a local hangout, so they realize you are not trying to cut them out of your life or treat them with less importance than your work. Be thoughtful but be firm. Remind them why you are on this Adventure. Let them know what's involved and why you need time to concentrate on your work.

- **Prolonged distractions:** Distractions brought on by a sick family member or by a pet in its last weeks of life are often the hardest to deal with. You just have to push through these difficult circumstances. Don't neglect your responsibilities to the family member or pet that needs your help, but keep your perspective and continue forward with your projects. You might go through a few days or weeks with less sleep than you are used to, but it's important to work through this time and not let it sidetrack you from your Adventure. You can make up for the lack of sleep when the crisis is over – and don't neglect the importance of doing that, because you need to maintain your own health too.

Obviously there are a many more areas and situations that might affect you. The key is simply to be aware of what is going on around you and to realize you should not play the martyr. Keep watch on yourself and listen to those who know you best.

You need to recognize how you affect people now

Earlier we discussed how others might react to your Adventure plans. This becomes even more the case when you are deep into your Adventure work and starting to see success. You will discover that people react very differently toward you when you do something out of the ordinary – even more so when they realize you are serious and committed to your new projects.

By your actions, you are demonstrating to those around you that you have the will to break out of your workday world and improve your financial situation. When you prove this consistently throughout the six weeks of your Adventure, reactions will grow stronger. Know what to expect and be prepared to keep things in perspective. Here is what I have encountered:

- **All-out supporters:** My parents are this way as are a

few friends. You will have your own cheering section of people who believe in what you are doing, who want to help and want to learn what you are learning. Be willing to share your progress with them. You might want to consider becoming a mentor as a future income stream. This cheerleading crowd is a great place to start. But remember to be humble and approach your mentoring relationship positively. Don't let ego and arrogance get in the way.

- **Doubting Thomases:** I have encountered people who say they wish that what I am doing could be done, but they know things don't really work this way. When you run into people like this, they will offer a mix of encouragement and caution. Take the encouragement and ignore the caution for the most part. What I have learned is that the old saying, "Those who say it can't be done are usually interrupted by those doing it," is usually very true.

- **Know-it-alls:** Some folks have tried to tell me what I am doing is a pipe dream. That I need to be more grounded. No doubt you will encounter people like this too. They will claim to know all there is to know about finances, but they are seldom rich. These are the heavy savers who are very good at managing money but don't take risks. They have good budgeting habits and you can certainly learn something about saving from them. But they will not do what is necessary to move ahead. While they might believe they have your best interests in mind, it is up to you to explain politely what you are doing and why. Then move on.

- **Naysayers:** As we discussed earlier, some people just don't want any part of what I am doing. These are the people you need to exercise the most caution with. They can become downright hostile in their attempts to tell you that what you are doing is wrong. You might need to sever your ties with them or at the very least, minimize your contact and avoid discussion of your Adventure with them.

Not only do you need to recognize and appreciate the affect you will have on people you already know. You must also realize that new people will come into your life as a result of your Adventure. You might meet people who want to follow your example. Some might want to partner with you and others might provide great resources. This new bounty of friendships and resources will offer you a lot of help and encouragement. Be prepared to accept it. You will find new teachers among this crowd as well.

Do not ignore your personal needs

Throughout this book, I have emphasized the importance of a balance between work and personal time. It would be a good idea if you actually write this down and review it as part of your week ending work. Maintaining time for yourself is critical to your success on this Adventure and beyond, and it's worth remembering particularly when you're deeply engaged in all your Adventure projects. It's easy to lose track of the need for personal time.

When you work for someone else, you work the expected hours then head home. Even if you are a workaholic, you make a distinction between work life and home life. While you are on this Adventure, the distinction easily becomes blurred – especially if your spouse is participating. The intensity and excitement that derives from this unique experience can cause you to lose perspective. You need to learn to carve out personal time throughout your Adventure.

Remember that these six weeks are a time for you to put systems into place that will sustain you beyond your Adventure. You are learning to live the life of your dreams. I'll bet that when you wrote down your dream lifestyle during your planning session, the life you imagined included plenty of free time. You need to learn habits now that will allow you to sustain this lifestyle in the future.

What if your Adventure work goes so well that you are able to leave your job and pursue your new income streams full time? That is great unless you achieved your success by sacrificing all other aspects of your life. If that is the case, you will continue to sacrifice and be miserable. Your new life will be just as limited as your old. You'll still be in a rut working around the clock for someone else: you! Your new life will not be the one you planned during your dreaming session.

The same holds true if you return to your job at the end of the six weeks. You will be more determined than ever to maintain the momentum of your Adventure. You know that if you don't keep the same pace going, you will never have the opportunity to leave your job for good. It's going to be hard enough to keep working your new income streams while you put in full days at work. If you developed those income streams by sacrificing your personal life, how much worse will it be when you return to that job?

It is better to take the Adventure a bit slower and keep your life in balance. This is hard when you first start out. You will be so enthusiastic and eager to get these new systems into place. You'll sense the clock ticking. Just remember that you are making changes that will last a lifetime. Dream your new lifestyle and start to live it now – completely. Use your schedule and do not cut out the personal and recreational time. They are there for a purpose!

April 1, 2003
Roger's journal entry

As befits all of us who are daring to get ahead, I am doing something for a favorite charity. I am building an infant's cradle with another woodworker friend of mine. I took most of today to work on it. If I could just figure out a way to make the money that I desire doing the woodworking.

At any rate, this helps me focus and I very much needed to do that today since I head back to work next week.

Remember the ten percent giving rule

One of the things I like about Mark Victor Hansen, Robert Allen and Brian Tracy among others is that they all emphasize that we are a part of a larger community and that it is important to give back a part of what we gain. Tithing is a term most often associated with religion but the principle is important regardless of your religious beliefs. If we are to be part of our community, we are compelled to return some of our money and/or time to help make things better in our lifetime.

I also believe that big givers are big receivers. "God blesses a generous giver" is a saying I have heard for years. I have found this to be true in my own life. The most generous people I know are truly the richest people I know.

****

It's good to have money
and the things that money can buy,
but it's good, too, to make sure
you haven't lost the things that money can't buy.
– George Horace Lorimer

PART IV

DISCOVERING THE REST OF YOUR LIFE
What happens next?

****

I do nothing but go about persuading you all,
old and young alike, not to take thought for your persons
or your properties, but and chiefly to care about
the greatest improvement of the soul.
I tell you that virtue is not given by money,
but that from virtue comes money
and every other good of man, public as well as private.
This is my teaching, and if this is the doctrine
which corrupts the youth, I am a mischievous person.
- Socrates, quoted by Plato, 'The Death of Socrates'

CHAPTER 11
REENTER YOUR WORLD AND CELEBRATE!

What we call 'creative work' ought not to be called work at all, because it isn't... I imagine that Thomas Edison never did a day's work in his last 50 years.
– Stephen Leacock

Choosing whether or not to return to your job...
If you do not need to return to your job after your Six Week Adventure, congratulations! You are ready to live your dream! But if you do, you can take steps to prepare for reentry to the world you left behind for six weeks. Remember, your return is only temporary. You have spent six weeks setting into place systems that will eventually allow you to leave your job permanently behind.

As you prepare for your reentry, you will not only want to get yourself back into the rhythm of your former work life. You will also need to put more effort into planning when you will leave your job for good. Stop and think about that for a moment. Your purpose in setting out on this Adventure was *to create the circumstances in which you can leave your job behind.* You need to envision that moment. You need to continue to work toward it. You need to project when your income streams will mature and what you require to keep that momentum going. Don't forget your long-term goals just because the Six Week Adventure ends.

Use the enthusiasm you've developed over the course of your Adventure to make realistically ambitious plans for the future. Give yourself a specific date to leave your job and plan out the schedule that will make that date a *reality*. Then prepare to hold yourself to those plans despite the impending distraction of your return to work. Do whatever it takes so that you don't forget your return to work is temporary. Don't go back to your old job, your familiar work environment and think nothing has really changed. *Everything* has changed and you will see that almost immediately.

In my situation, I had to return to work temporarily. The idea of returning to my job felt a bit strange, because I had grown so much during the six weeks. But I felt we needed to work our streams for a while before I left my job permanently. I wanted to keep our insurance coverage and a few other benefits a little while longer. Besides, my salary remained a comfort for Marita. While she is fully behind this project, she is more cautious than I am and didn't want us to rush.

I needed to figure out how to keep the momentum of our Adventure going after I returned to my job. Toward the end of the six weeks, Marita and I started to formulate new goals to get more out of our income streams. We looked harder at tangible results too. We set our sights on a specific income. We realized that we might not see $1 million net worth by summer 2003 but agreed that by the end of 2003, this net worth was a realistic goal. With that goal in mind, we planned what we would need to do to keep this momentum going.

We planned how we would work the various systems after I returned to my job. I partnered with my parents on the Real Estate work. Meanwhile, I started to wake up at my normal work hour and started to catch up on professional reading to prepare for reentry to my workplace.

If I had doubted I could keep the momentum going,

I wouldn't have returned to work. But I knew I could, because I believed in what we were doing and loved doing it. I had gained a lot of confidence over the six weeks and felt excited that things were falling into place. Our new income streams were working and I knew we had to keep them going.

I also knew a layoff was pending at my company. I had no choice but to keep the Adventure rolling because I knew that soon, those streams would be my only source of income. Even if the layoff didn't come quickly, we decided I would leave my job as soon as our new systems started to earn more than my salary. We kept a tentative date in mind of fall 2003.

It was easy for me to have a positive attitude returning to work, because I returned to a welcoming environment. My fellow employees were very understanding of what I had done. They asked a lot of questions. I could tell our conversations were eye opening for many of them. It was amazing to realize that while I had changed so much, they had not.

The first few days back at work, I felt really distracted. My emotions ran between excitement over the Adventure I had just completed and disappointment that I couldn't continue to focus on my new income streams full time. Every day that I was back at my job, I couldn't help but think I was underpaid! Every minute represented time I could not spend doing things I knew would produce greater returns.

April 1, 2003
Marita's journal entry

It is hard to believe it is already April and this is the final week of our six-week adventure. It has had its ups and downs but it has been good.

Today I looked at the eight Stocks on hand. Seven of the call options I am going to wait on. Four still continue to show a loss but the loss is still above 50%. Three of the Stocks have stayed the same.

I did sell the options on MSFT – Microsoft. This is a put option and looks like the trend of the Stock is to go up. So I made a profit of fifty dollars.

I added another Stock: STJ – St. Jude Med. It was a little more than my standard so I purchased 500 shares instead of my usual 1, 000. Both the seven-day and 30-day lines are trending up.

By the time a few weeks passed and I got back into the swing, I realized how much I had grown beyond my job. I felt a huge degree of confidence. We had done a great deal and were in a position to do great things in the future. Just reflecting on that, I knew my current job was the least profitable of all my income streams. That realization gave me the determination to stay focused on my new streams in my free time. I work these streams a few hours each day after work and listen to tapes in the car. We are definitely making headway and using every day to prepare for my permanent departure from my job.

Returning to work did have one downside in that I was thrust back into a much more negative environment. I really felt for the first-line management in particular, because they had a heavy burden in terms of impending layoffs. My boss was really under stress. But I was able to keep a positive outlook despite the environment, because I was jazzed for the future Marita and I were headed for.

When you reenter your workplace, you will feel that confidence. You will feel empowered and ready to leave your job for good, just as soon as you are able. If you continue to work your new income streams, that time will come quickly.

Meanwhile, you will have to deal with a new set of distractions. Just remember that the concept of distraction isn't new. More than likely, you've had to deal with distractions throughout your Adventure. You've had to be creative in order to deal with obstacles and set up new systems from scratch. You already have the momentum you need. You just have to keep it going. Apply to the post-Adventure world the same creativity you used to develop and carry out your Six Week Adventure, and you'll keep pushing forward.

This is where partnerships and the efficient use of time become critical. Don't be afraid to share your good fortune with partners whose time you can leverage at minimal cost. And look for those free periods of time in your daily schedule when you can continue to work your income streams.

Your mental outlook is important too. Approach your return to work with a positive frame of mind. For now, your job provides the income you need to keep your new income streams going. And the situation is only temporary. Soon you will be able to leave your job and live off the new systems you set up during your Adventure.

Use the time you have now to plan for that. Part of your post-Adventure responsibility is to be reasonable and sensible in nurturing your new income streams. Take full advantage of the time you have left at your job to prepare for the day you will leave. When that day comes, you will know you are leaving for something much better!

It's easy to become impatient, to want to break free and continue to work your new income systems full time. This is why your end-of-Adventure planning is so critical. Give yourself a roadmap and timetable to follow that will help you stay positive and focused. Mark your calendar with the date you anticipate leaving your job. Just seeing that date will help you keep things in perspective.

I cannot deny that going back to work after the Adventure will be hard. But it can also be a great opportunity. Your full-time job provides some great benefits while you

From the Newsletter
Roger Mallory

Over the last few weeks, I have encountered several brushes with people about the issue of professionalism. It has caused me to think about what that word really means. In fact, it has been a search within me, a journey, if you will, for the essence of professionalism. Here is what I have discovered so far.

- Professionalism is not about telling other people how to behave. Over the years I have been told by countless people that there are certain ways to behave in a "professional" manner. I have found this advice to be true most of the time, but it is also true I would have acted appropriately in that situation anyway! All this kind of advice does is demean a person.

- Professionalism is about modeling. Converse to the first point, the best and truest professionals I have been privileged to know say nothing about being professional. They simply are. One of my mentors is a good example. The first time he met my wife and me, this fellow was incredibly friendly and courteous, even though I was not that friendly or presentable. It was that single act that assured me

are working your income streams: a salary that provides living income, insurance that isn't insanely expensive, and retirement accounts. Your work environment also puts you in contact with potential customers, partners and mentors. The reality is that you make your world what it is. So why not make it the best!

Celebrate your accomplishments

A priest and a rabbi operated a church and a synagogue across the street from each other. Since their schedules intertwined, they decided to go in together to buy a car.

After the purchase, they drove it home and parked it on the street between them.

A few minutes later, the rabbi looked out and saw the priest sprinkling water on their new car. It didn't need a wash, so he hurried out and asked the priest what he was doing.
"I'm blessing it, " the priest replied.

I had done well to pursue that relationship.

- Professionalism is not about a set of "universal standards." While it is true there are things that are considered "professional" in most business settings, it can vary a great deal. Take dress for example. While we have, in this newsletter, discussed appropriate attire, we have not said any "thou shalts" or "thou shalt nots" about what a person should wear. And Crystal was right not to do that. If any of you have ever visited Microsoft, you can see the range of professional dress very easily. In many places, casual dress is perfectly acceptable. However, go to the Human Resources or Sales departments and you will think you have entered a whole different company. The point is that "rules" of behavior and dress vary widely and really do not define professionalism.

- Professionalism is about being "others centered." As I said in the first paragraph, I have had a number of discussions concerning professionalism, professional behavior and all manner of different issues about being professional. So I started to think about those I have dealt with over the years and started to wonder about the one thing that

The rabbi considered this a moment, then went back inside the synagogue. He reappeared a moment later with a hacksaw, walked over to the back of the car and cut two inches off the tailpipe.
– Anonymous

Ladies and Gentlemen, it is vital to remember that rites of passage need to be celebrated. Americans are terrible at this. We seem to think celebration is a relic of religious traditions rather than an acknowledgement of a deep human yearning. Celebration is the act of marking the way we have come on life's path. We celebrate because we are alive! Though I believe religion enhances the experience, celebration is not about religion. It is about becoming a better, more rounded and successful person.

Why should you celebrate? Because you have a reason to! You have successfully completed the Six Week Adventure. It's a big deal, folks!

We celebrated by going to Las Vegas to a seminar that was a dream experience for me. We had a wonderful time. Here's what we celebrated:

caused me to view them as professional. Two things struck me about all of them. The first was that they had the ability to teach and model their professionalism to others. The second was their ability to always focus on the customer or person they were dealing with at the time. A professional boss can deal with even the most difficult cases and at the end let an employee feel s/he was cared for. A professional salesperson addresses the needs of the person and not the needs of "the sale." Amazingly, such a salesperson will have to close the sale much less often because he has built trust!

Certainly this is not nearly a complete definition of professionalism, but it gets the idea across. It is my belief that professionalism is about who you are whenever you are in a professional situation. You can be respectful, dressed appropriately, say the right words and have impeccable manners. But if you cannot engender confidence that you are serious then you are wasting time.

To me, this is why we need mentors. I encourage each person reading this newsletter to regularly meet with people who are professionals and model the traits that have made them successful!

- A successful Adventure
- The purchase of our investment house, as detailed in our journal
- Meeting a number of key contacts and new friends
- Our Tax Lien investment success
- Marita's personal growth
- The start of our new lives with multiple sources of income
- Our future
- Everything else worthy of celebration

Likewise, we will celebrate my layoff with a few friends at a local restaurant!

Document your lessons

In the world of project management, one of the documents that is supposed to be developed is something called "Lessons Learned." An old saying goes, "Those who do not learn from the mistakes of the past are doomed to failure." If you document the lessons you learned, you will know what to do and what not to do. Thus you will be able to learn the right things to practice and the wrong things that you need to avoid.

I have a list on my computer that I contribute to periodically. I review it every time I open it. I am notorious for not documenting things. The Adventure has reformed me in this area, and I find this documentation enormously helpful. I advise you to get used to learning from your own experiences as well as the experiences of others.

One of the best Real Estate gurus and public speakers I have encountered is John Childers. At a recent seminar, he said, "Perfect practice makes perfect." In other words, practice does you no good if you practice the wrong things! If you know what the wrong things are, you can avoid them. Thus I make it my business to know what does not work well. That's just as important as knowing what does work well.

Review your Adventure and plan for your future

Every week, I like to read a little about our Adventure! It grounds me and reminds me what I need to do to maintain the momentum. This exercise isn't about looking back. It's about looking forward and remembering where we are headed.

This is another reason it's so important that you keep a journal to document your Adventure. Writing this book is a way for me to keep the past in mind as I look to the future. You can do the same by continuing to write in your journal and dream book.

As you remind yourself where you are going, it's important that you continue to plan, just as you did during the six weeks. Certain things need to be planned in order to keep your momentum. Continue to set goals and write down your dreams. Seek assistance from your spouse and family. Plan to work your new income streams after hours and on the weekend. You need to make even more of an effort now to schedule free time to relax. It will become just as important as it is scarce. Don't forget that you are human. Burning out will not help you maintain your momentum.

Reality is a non-relenting master at times. You have only 24 hours in a day so it is best to optimize that time. You can work during your lunch hour, but be careful not to do anything that would give your employer a reason to claim ownership of your hard work. Use a cell phone or pay phone for calls and don't leave anything on an office computer. Make use of your commute time by listening to instructional CDs and tapes.

You will find ways to work your income streams around your full-time job because after the six weeks ends, these streams will be an important part of your life. And they will be your keys to leaving your job permanently behind.

****

Well done is better than well said.
- Benjamin Franklin

****

Dost thou love life?
Then do not squander time,
for that's the stuff life is made of.
- Benjamin Franklin

CHAPTER 12
MASTERING YOUR SYSTEMS FOR THE LONG HAUL

Our attitudes control our lives. Attitudes are a secret power working 24 hours a day, for good or bad. It is of paramount importance that we know how to harness and control this great force.
– Tom Blandi

Review the seven secrets

Lessons are not lessons unless they are remembered. As you review the seven secrets of success, you will recognize accomplishments that were the direct result of these secrets. Even if you do not yet see results, you will notice a change in yourself as you review these secrets. These keys will help solidify what you have learned on your Adventure. Review them when the Adventure is over and continue to review them in the future.

One example of how Secret 6 helped us: We have made very nice returns on our ongoing investments in Tax Liens. We accomplished this by dealing with naysayers. Over and over, people told us Tax Liens were a lot more risky than they are. The real reason more people don't take advantage of them is that people do not like auctions.

The seven secrets provide a framework that allows us to be secure in how we approach everything we do financially. As you learn to be creative, these seven secrets will become part of the way you think. The more I practice the things I learned as I wrote this book and moved beyond our Adventure, the more I realized that all successful business people are in the business of creating. Microsoft creates software, Kraft creates food products, Boeing creates airplanes, 3M creates post-it notes, and so on. What do you create?

As you move forward, you will need to be a creator. The seven secrets will help you get there. Succeeding in the entrepreneurial world is about doing things that work. These seven secrets are things wealthy people do to succeed! Are you ready to take another look at them?

- **Work smarter for greater results**
- **Enthusiasm can make miracles**
- **Concentration and focus can make the difference**
- **Engage your family and friends with your dreams**
- **Allow your life to change**
- **Deal with the Big Four obstacles:** naysayers, cash, personal difficulties, external distractions and world events
- **Learn what it takes to get there**

April 2, 2003
Marita's journal entry

Good news: the Stock market is up! I waited until after lunch to look at my Stocks and made some changes.

I sold HSY, PCAR, TEVA and BLL for profits totaling $3, 700. Another Stock, ZHM I sold at a loss of $1, 300. This sale was hard to do because it appears to have some indication that it may be going up. However, this Stock has lost 51% of my money, so I decided to sell. I will keep this Stock on my watch list to see what happens and perhaps gain some more knowledge of the Stock market.

I am still looking at Microsoft, which I sold yesterday. It was a good thing I did because the Stock did go up. Remember, I had a put option on it.

Now I have three Stocks in my paper trading. I am waiting on these to see what changes happen tomorrow. At this time so much is going on that I am content to keep practicing my skills on paper trading.

Develop new routines and goals

For the first few weeks after I reentered my "regular world," things still moved forward under the momentum we created during our Adventure. As the weeks passed, however, Marita and I realized we needed to make some changes to keep these good things going. Here is what we did to refocus on the long run:

- **We reprioritized our social life.** We hang out with friends who are supportive and have similar interests. Some friends are just too negative. Also, remember that the average American represents the average income among his/her circle of friends and acquaintances. This may sound cold, but if you want to up your income, one of the surest ways is to hang out with wealthier people. Quantity is important. Get to know more people. Earlier in the book we listed some great places to start. Take advantage of them!

- **We set aside certain evenings to do work.** Marita is the lead contractor on the renovations for our investment properties and I contribute part of the labor.

- **We hired people to do some of the work.** We have a wonderful friend who is doing our yard work and we also have a newsletter editor. When your business starts hopping, here is a list of services you might want to hire out. The services you need will depend on the types of projects you are doing and which tasks you would rather not do yourself:

  - Webmaster
  - Newsletter editor
  - Painter
  - Gardener
  - Housekeeper
  - Ghostwriter
  - Editor
  - Bookkeeper
  - Computer consultant
  - Mailing expert

- **We continued to go to seminars and classes and to participate in other types of learning.** Over the two months that followed the six weeks, we attended two major training seminars and we are the better for them. The commitment is major so take what you can. I recommend participating in a major training seminar one to four times a year.

- **We continued to attend industry-specific events.** We are interested in publishing and selling our books, so we went to the Book Expo America (BEA) that occurs every year at the end of May. If you are interested in publishing a book, go to this. If you are interested in computers, go to COMDEX. If you are interested in electronics, go to the Consumer Electronics Show (CES), and so on. Learn form those who have gone before you!

- **We took care of ourselves spiritually.** We go to church, read inspirational literature and listen to inspirational recordings. I find it helpful to receive inspirational quotes from several websites. They get me pumped for the day to come. The two I enjoy most are **www.briantracy.com** and **www.nightingale.com**. Whatever way you do it, pay attention to this part of your life!

- **We were optimistically realistic.** We all want our new lives to begin yesterday. The truth is that, like a building skyscraper, you are in this for the long haul. Design your new life and live intentionally with purpose and patience.

- **We learned patience.** While this is not my long suit, fortunately it is Marita's. We are successful because I am the dreamer and she is the pragmatist. Two important lessons here: learn from your weaknesses and learn patience.

- **We practiced a successful attitude.** Read the quote by Tom Blandi at the beginning of this chapter. There are many secrets to learning how to harness a successful attitude. The most successful for me has been this: Practice the way you want to be, and you will become it. If you want to have a bad attitude, practice it. If you want a successful attitude, practice that. With every idea you have, practice believing it will work. Rather than looking for reasons as to why it won't work, search out the reasons why it will!

- **We kept our focus.** Don't allow outside distractions to take undue precedence in your life. Deal with life, with its unexpected turns and distractions. Through it all, stay focused. Again, practice is the key here!

- **We set a specific goal for when I would leave my job.** You should do the same. See if you can make this a financial rather than a time-based goal, e.g., you will leave your job when your income exceeds "x" amount of dollars. Even so, it's good to put a date on your calendar, so you can see exactly what you're shooting for. Otherwise you might be tempted to delay. For those of us facing a layoff, the goals can be financial as well but more connected to time. We hope that we will be financially viable before our benefits run out. This situation is more dire but no less important. Goals are part of a successful life. Use them!

These 11 steps will help you move forward ambitiously yet realistically. Think of your post-Adventure world as a longer Adventure that is just beginning. Learn to manage your time and take a positive approach. Settle in for the long haul. After all, this is to become your new way of life. The Six Week Adventure and the months that follow are not a race. You plan carefully, set things in motion and work your new income streams to generate income over the long term. Stick to it and you will see immediate results but, more importantly, you'll be able to map out an even more successful future.

As I mentioned earlier in this book, one of your biggest potential obstacles to changing your life is fear. Only through confidence and commitment will you overcome those fears. If you fear that your changes won't really work, they won't. If you approach them with a positive mindset, however, they will work. Your journey over the six weeks will give you this confidence and you will retain it when you go back to your "normal" world. You will realize how much you have changed. But it won't hurt to reaffirm the changes you've made.

Remember what you have just finished celebrating. You had the courage and fortitude to change your life and move on to the things you love and want to do. One reason I encourage you to celebrate and document is so that you will have a concrete reminder of your achievements.

If you remember your celebration, if you use what you have learned on a regular basis, and if you continue to learn new things, you will reaffirm your new life changes. Teaching others what you have learned is also a great way to reaffirm your accomplishments and hang on to that new confidence. Already people around me have

April 3, 2003
Roger's journal entry

Today started out wrong. Our dog died. I woke up early and went to the kitchen and she was lying there as she always does, but she just didn't wake up. Chelsea was a great little dog who, over the last ten years was there for me when I needed a little cheering up. I will miss her a great deal!

Later my father joined me for my trip to Oly-mpia to look for Real Estate. To this point the hunt has been with an agent and we did come across a number of interesting possibilities.
I am going to send a couple of offers down there over the weekend and see if I can buy any or all of three properties. At the same time, I want to get a look at the FSBOs down there. More and more, I am finding that I want to deal directly with the seller rather than an agent if I can.

On the way home from Olympia, my father and I discussed the future of our ventures together. I am hopeful that we will partner on some future projects and that he can do some of the searching that I can't do at this time. I think this will work out just fine!

started their own Adventures, and their achievements reinforce my own. One of my friends has already surpassed me in the Real Estate game and it looks like I will learn a great deal from him!

At times you will start to feel that you are back in your old ways. We all have these feelings and, ironically, they bring about as much fear as when you were unsure you could make these changes. That's okay! It happens. But when it does, remember this: You succeeded! You did! You took the chances, made the decisions and made things happen. Your achievements cannot be taken away. You are the better for them.

Revise your one-page business plan

As you move on, your business will mature. You will probably want to incorporate and make other appropriate changes. Add these changes into your business plan.

A business plan helps you focus and stay on course. It is a great tool for keeping your business in line. It does not need to be lengthy, as long as your plan focuses on every aspect of your business and how you will achieve your goals.

When your business gets big enough, you might need to present your plan to an investor or banker. This book is a great place to start: ***Small Business for Dummies, 2nd edition***, by Eric Tyson and Jim Schell.

We formed an LLC, as we will discuss in the next chapter. Not only did we modify our business plan to reflect this change. We also expanded our business plan to take a longer view with a wider scope. Our plan now reflects our business-oriented goals list.

Automate everything you can

As we have discussed all along, it's wise to set up your streams so they will run themselves eventually. Hopefully you have thought about this from the beginning. But in the post-Adventure world, you need to give even more thought to automating your business. This is important whether or not you have to go back to your full-time job.

Kiyosaki refers to this concept of automation in a number of his books. To increase your financial independence and success, you need income from vehicles you do not need to attend to all the time. As you grow your business, you will be able to hire managers and other employees to do the work for you. Until then, here are some helpful ways to automate your income streams:

- **Get a website.** It is a great way to do just about any business. Once your website is up and running, it can earn you money 24/7 with very little effort on your part. We use our website www.anbeyond.com for communications. Mass communication is so easy with this tool. One letter can be sent to thousands of people. We are also retooling our website to do a big chunk of our marketing and order processing.

- **If the Stock Market is one of your streams, consider an online broker service.** Be sure you get one that comes with a human being you can talk to, in case you encounter problems.
  A number of good online broker services are out there. Marita uses one and has found it helpful in automating that income stream.

- **Hire people to do the work you do not have time for.** Obviously this depends on your budget. But start thinking about it even before you can afford it, so that you'll know exactly what you are looking for and when. It takes time to find the right person for the job, so don't wait until you can afford it to start looking. Barter arrangements can also be successful, as long as you're careful to stipulate the terms in a written document – just as you would any other contract relationship.

- **Use secretarial and postal processing services.** You'll find it's not only faster but cheaper to pay someone who specializes in these services than to do everything yourself. One good place to turn is a virtual assistant service. Organizations such as the International Virtual Assistants Association at www.ivaa.org offer a free online RFP service where you can post your job and take bids from certified virtual assistants who are qualified to help you. This is contract work with people who run their own businesses supporting people like you. Rather than having to go through the paperwork and expense of hiring employees, you pay the virtual assistants for the work they do, just as you would any other service vendor. You can spend your time on projects that generate much more income than you will spend on these services.

Automating helps you focus on developing your business. The more you can automate and farm out, the more you are free to do the higher value things you need to build your business. You can spend time learning new things, creating your next project and expanding your goals. Automation also allows you to give more time to worthy causes and do the things you enjoy.

April 4, 2003
Roger's journal entry

Today is the last weekday of the adventure. It is also the first full day I have without my dog. Ahhh, kind of a downer, but it was a productive day. First, I did my due diligence on the houses I looked at on Thursday. They are very interesting but they are all too expensive at this point. I will send along some offers, but I doubt I will receive any response. At the same time, however, it is good practice.

I also worked on the outline for the book that we are going to publish documenting our six weeks. I am excited to see where this thing goes! I love writing, but the time thing is just not there at this point. Maybe if I can buy another house, we will start to have the equity position to do some interesting and fun things!

I also spent some time today researching asset protection stuff. It should be very interesting. I do have a call into a rather large company in Las Vegas that sets up corporations. I look forward to hearing from them in the near future.

After all, those are important reasons you took the Six Week Adventure in the first place.

Another cool thing that comes from the automation process is that you create opportunities for others! You aid the businesses whose help you enlist. You enrich the community where your vendors and associates live by helping their dreams come true. In essence, by doing business with others to help automate and streamline your own business, you create wealth and prosperity for far more people than just yourself. Not a bad way to do business, is it?

Continue to enlist partners

As you move into the post-Adventure world, remember to enlist the help of family, friends and new associates. This is an ongoing process, one that for the most successful entrepreneurs never ends. Continue to socialize, to seek mentors and to learn. The more people you meet, the more opportunities you will encounter. And the more you will reinforce what you have learned. Networking is a great way to keep your momentum going.

Networking is not only the most effective way to launch your business. It's a necessary part of business development. It needs to become a regular part of working your new income streams. I started networking before I began the Six Week Adventure and I continue to focus on networking every day.

Successful people know successful people and they meet new ones constantly.

Things you can do weekly to maintain your momentum

If you've been following this chapter carefully, you probably have a very long to-do list by now. The number of things you need to do in your post-Adventure world can become overwhelming. Here are five simple habits you can develop that will help you stay on course:

- **Review and revise your goals.** Goal setting is useless unless you use and review your goals on a regular basis. The short goal setting primer included in Appendix II offers a good method to accomplish this. Regardless of whether or not you use our plan or someone else's, be sure to put your goal list into action and review it regularly. This action keeps you looking ahead. It helps you stay creative and focused and allows you to expand your possibilities.

- **Read at least half a book every week.** Half a book is only a suggestion. Whatever amount you choose – 10 pages a day, a book a week – be sure to stick to that amount and read regularly. Alternate between informational and inspirational books. Stay well rounded.

- **Listen to tapes in your car.** Audiotapes provide a great way to supplement your reading and expand your mind. I usually listen to the news first on my morning commute. As soon as I get through that, I pop in the audiotape I want to listen to.

- **Set a goal to meet someone new every week.** People are the key to your success. Sticking to this goal helps me move out of my comfort zone a bit and affords me the opportunity to expand my circle of resources. Besides, it is fun to meet and get to know new people. Special events, chambers of commerce, Rotary, church, and Toastmasters are just some of the places where you can make these contacts.

- **Remember to take some fun time.** One emphasis of this book has been to stay well rounded in your business and personal life. When I neglect to take time for myself, I become too serious and ornery! I also start to doubt myself. Take some time out and don't regret it. Know that it's all part of your plan. Enjoy it!

The sooner you make these a habit, the more a part of your life they will become. The better chance you will have to maintain the momentum of your Adventure. These five simple things are not too much to ask of yourself, even when reality gets in the way. Make them a habit – a natural part of your day just like eating and breathing – and you will not neglect them no matter what else comes up.

You'll notice, too, that these five steps keep you in touch with your project. After a rough day at work, you'll feel invigorated if you come home at night and add something new to your business plan, sketch out a new project or listen to an audiotape. This action will take you away from the world of your job and remind you that you have another life in motion. Things are moving forward and one day soon you will leave that job!

It will help also to remember your starting point. Read your journal and follow your own progress through the Adventure. Review your initial expectations and achievements. Remember that your expectations have grown along with you. Don't dampen your enthusiasm but don't let your new expectations frustrate you either. As you review your progress and update your plans, you'll realize how much you have achieved... and how much momentum you have going.

April 5, 2003
Roger's journal entry

So this is our last day. Marita is at a church retreat and I am home alone. Most of the day was spent working around the house, getting it fit in the case we decide to move to the other house. A buddy of mine came over for a few hours this afternoon.

All in all the day was quite relaxing. The afternoon and evening were spent working on the book outline and on plans for how the website will look in future. One of our big projects is to move our site to another hosting company. Our current provider is just not doing the trick!

I know this entry is kind of anticlimactic, but to me it is a time for beginning. I don't see a need to be too dramatic about any of it. So...

Thank you all for all the support!

CHAPTER 13

YOU ARE ON YOUR WAY!

Going Where You Never Thought You Could

The big challenge is to become all
that you have the possibility of becoming.
You cannot believe what it does to the human spirit
to maximize your human potential
and stretch yourself to the limit.
- Jim Rohn

Before we go on to discuss some of the major sources of income in the Epilogue, I want to mention to you in parting what you can do to ensure your success with whatever streams you choose. Learn a "can do" attitude. When an opportunity arises, try to figure out how it can be done rather than dwelling on the reasons it might be difficult to accomplish. Perhaps it won't work out, but you don't know that until you try every possible way to work through the problems.

Confusing? Not really. Simply put, you can choose to succeed or you can choose not to. The choice is yours. Choose the "can do" road. Persist, be patient and you will succeed. And keep these three things in mind as you read about the various income sources:

You can continue to create

New ideas are now your life! As we went through the Adventure, I puzzled over one thing: how do I apply the skills and talents I developed over the years to my new-found approach to financial independence and wealth building? Thus came this book. I love the written word and over the years I have written several hundred academic papers, sermons and workshops. Doing this book has been a way to release that creative energy to broaden my sources of income.

From the book idea came the idea to do a seminar, workbook and home study courses. Still farther down the road, I look forward to writing two more books that I have in mind already. Who knows what will come next! Once you are in the mindset to create your future, you will become an idea machine. *Always* write down your ideas as you think of them and address them one at a time as you go along. You will be surprised how many people really want to buy what you are interested in.

You can go as far as you allow yourself to go

In ***Think and Grow Rich***, Hill discusses 16 characteristics of success that you can learn. Read them! If you apply yourself to learning in your specific areas of interest, if you exercise the heart and endurance, and if you apply yourself to your team, you are on your way to wherever you allow yourself to go. A few years ago I was single, had a second-rate job that I was about to lose through a layoff, and I had a negative net worth. After learning from so many wise people, I discovered that my future is my business and it is what I make of it.

The result? We are doing quite well with our new strategies and we are getting close to our first major financial goal. This is just the first step on our way to where we want to go. Marita and I want to reach a point financially where we can give the vast majority of our

Our goals and how we did:

1. Buy two investment properties: We bought one, but its value was well beyond what we thought we would get for two. We feel this is a very successful part of the adventure!

2. Launch a website and a regular newsletter. These things both happened! We are excited about the growth we have experienced and we are looking to do some exciting things in the coming weeks and months!

3. Find a writer to help us write our book. We have found a super one and the book is now in progress.

4. Do the paper trading and make our first trade by the end of the first six weeks. Marita has done extremely well, but given the volatility of the current environment ***(editors note: This entry reflects the market as of May 2003)*** she has chosen to wait a bit. I expect she will do the first trade within the next few weeks.

Eleven things we learned that are essential to the success of a project like this:

1. Attitude is very important!
2. Don't quit. Success takes perseverance.
3. Learn to prioritize.
4. Make family a priority.
5. Make a plan and follow it.
6. Dream big. Shoot for the stars!
7. Delegate as much as you can afford.
8. Pay attention to the big picture.
9. Trust yourself.
10. Make learning a priority and a habit.
11. Be nice and learn patience.

Today I learned a hard lesson about the last item listed here. I was very inconsiderate to a clerk at a local establishment. The lady behind me tried to correct me in a very condescending way. She was wrong to approach it the way she did, but she was right about the way I was behaving. I must admit that when I am fatigued and frustrated, I need to be doubly alert to what I do and say.

I would wager there is something in the above list for each of us to work on. I look forward to being a much better customer the next time I am at that store.

income to worthy causes. I know we will get there if we just keep working the streams we set in motion during our Adventure.

What do you want and how far do you want to go? At this point you know what it will take. And you know you can do it!

You can give as much as you want to make a better world.

This book is about financial success and freedom. It is not about becoming a greedy miser. Giving is a responsibility that should make you ecstatic. Here are the five areas I mentioned earlier where you can apply your giving:

- **Give of your money.** We tithe on a consistent basis.
- **Give of your possessions.** Every year we try to give specific items – furniture, food and housewares – to the less fortunate.
- **Give of your time.** Marita and I volunteer at church and through other organizations.
- **Give of your talents.** I love woodworking and every year I work on a different project for a local charity auction.
- **Give of your knowledge.** This is a particular talent that deserves its own category. Accountants, investors and just about any other professional or skilled worker can provide knowledge to charitable causes.

We give regularly to our church. This might seem mundane to some and irrelevant to others, but we have found a wonderful support system that has returned to us immeasurably in kindness. Our church provides effective community assistance. I believe our giving in all five of the above categories has made a difference. More than that, giving puts into perspective your life and how you live it.

At this point, it seems like we have dumped a lot of information on you. If you've read this far, you are no doubt excited about the possibility of doing your own Adventure. But you probably still wonder: Does it really work? Did it work for us?

My answer is a resounding yes! Throughout this book, I have given you ideas and strategies to move forward with your financial future. I have shared my successes with you. These successes continue! Our future is bright. We have done well with the Real Estate investments and our Stock portfolio is growing. Our Tax Lien certificate investments are doing well and our new projects show promise.

The last proof of success I will offer is perhaps the strongest. Some of our friends have joined in this Adventure based on our success. While I can't share names or strategies, I can tell you we know several people who are pursuing Real Estate and other streams as a result of seeing our success. When you complete your Adventure, you will discover you have the same effect on those around you, with good reason. You will be on your way to achieving lifelong financial independence. You will be a model for others to follow!

April 7, 2003
Marita's journal entry

Is this the beginning or is this the end? The six-week adventure is over yet we are still in the midst of our beginnings. I continue to do my paper trading on Stocks. I find that lately I have been doing better at trading options. I need to study more about it.

Roger has gone back to work at Boeing. The goal is to get him out of there. Perhaps that is the next part of our adventure. Tomorrow we will be in contact with our ghost-writer for our book. Again, maybe that is the next part of our adventure.

During this six-week adventure we have had many opportunities for being upbeat even in the midst of war, adoption worries, our grandmother's illness and the death of Chelsea, our dog.

This is a beginning to put forth effort in our dreams and live up to our goals. We are doing the do instead of just the wishes. I am excited about the next steps we do in our adventures.

So here you are. You have read the book, maybe started your preparations and you are wondering if this is the real thing or just another book about becoming a rich person. Well, that is really up to you! In this book, we have given you some great tools. We have referred you to dozens of sources and we have shown you how we did it. We hope that you will take these tools and apply them to a prosperous future that is a positive influence in your life and the lives around you. We hope that you now have a framework on which you will build a strong and prosperous business that is fulfilling and rewarding. A tall order, you say? Maybe, but we know that you are up to it!

You see, the real secret to this is found in two qualities that you have already demonstrated by reading this far. First, you have persevered and found the energy to read this book to the end. Secondly, you have demonstrated that you can create. Everything that is sold and bought is created by someone. Throughout this book, we have attempted to help you create strategies, tools and relationships for your future. You are already well on your way to that promising new horizon.

So take heart. Harness that excitement that you have for your future and all that it holds. And along the way, I would love to hear about your successes at rogermallory@anbeyond.com. Good Luck and God Bless!

****

There are powers inside of you,
which, if you could discover and use,
would make of you everything
you ever dreamed or imagined you could become.
- Orison Swett Marden

EPILOGUE
MULTIPLE SOURCES FOR YOUR ADVENTURE
A List of Business and Money Making Opportunities

Throughout this book, I have avoided addressing in detail two subjects: marketing and specific sources of income. This was intentional because this is not a book devoted to either of these areas. The purpose of this book is to get you started on your way to a financial future that is secure and affords you the freedom you desire. To help you get started, however, I want to address marketing and specific sources of income here briefly.

First, let's address marketing. If you are going to pursue any strategy that involves selling a product or service, you will need to think about marketing at some point. Direct marketing and publicity are the bread and butter of the small entrepreneur's selling strategy. I am still learning these things and recommend that you do your own research. However, let me recommend the following to get you started:

Denise Michaels at **www.denisemichaels.com**. You can learn a lot from Denise's one-of-a-kind marketing mind. She is very busy and I have not yet attended one of her seminars. But I have heard nothing but exceptional reports about her teaching. Not only that, but the price is a real winner! As of this writing, nothing out there comes close.

Dian Thomas at **www.milliondollarpr.com/**. Dian has more than a decade of national television experience on shows such as *The Today Show* on NBC and ABC's *Home* show. Her publicity program is great for beginner and pro alike, and it's well worth the hefty price!

I've found the whole ***Guerrilla Marketing*** series from Jay Conrad Levinson to be very helpful. The original is great. I also like the ***Guerilla Publicity*** book that Levinson wrote along with Jill Lublin and Rick Frishman. If you read that book in conjunction with Dian's materials, you will become a publicity machine!

Another great resource is George Brown's online branding services. George works in conjunction with Rick Frishman to help infopreneurs market their products: **www.onlinebranding.info**. He also offers seminars to help small businesses with branding:
www.all-about-training.com.

You'll find a wealth of marketing material on the Internet. I am still doing research and have a lot to learn. My recommendation is that you do a lot of research, ask questions and see what works for your projects.

Now let's talk about income streams. You will find literally hundreds of ways to pursue your income streams. What follows are 12 sources of income I believe offer you opportunities that are immediately accessible. This section is intended as a way to pique your interest. I cannot offer a specific recommendation or endorsement, because you need to decide what works for you. Rather, look at this section as a way of starting out on your own research for your Adventure!

CONSERVATIVE INVESTING

I believe this is a must. You might have heard the adage that says you should invest your age as percentage of your assets into conservative vehicles and use the rest for higher-risk opportunities. If you are 40, this means you would put 40 percent of your assets into savings, bonds, annuities and other safe investments while you invest the other 60 percent in higher-risk vehicles. While I am not a financial advisor and this is just my opinion, I do have a formula I prefer. I always put at least 50 percent into the safe vehicles, 20 percent into the higher-risk opportunities and the balance into medium-risk investments. You need a 401K and an IRA to start and go from there. It is very important that you get a financial advisor. You won't regret that decision.

You will find many opportunities for all three degrees of investments. The next twelve income streams will offer some interesting answers to your needs. Robert Allen provides a great discussion of this in his book ***Multiple Streams of Income: How to Generate a Lifetime of Unlimited Wealth***. This book is a great way to start your research on income streams. The first four chapters are particularly important. If you read nothing else from that book, read those chapters.

REAL ESTATE

You will discover a number of ways to make money in Real Estate. I want to list just a few here. I can't do justice to any Real Estate strategy with the brief discussion that follows. I just want to make you aware of some of your options. If anything appeals to you, I recommend that you look into those opportunities in much greater detail. John Childer's free class at **www.johnchilders.com** is a great place to start. Bernie Zick at **www.zick.com** also offers some great materials that will provide you with a solid introduction to Real Estate investing.

Here are some of the Real Estate options available:

Flipping houses

This is the easiest strategy to understand. You search for bargains and then resell them at a profit. You'll find a number of attractive ways to pursue this option using nothing-down strategies. Robert Allen's book, ***Nothing Down for the 90's*** is probably the most popular text on this subject, but check out Childer's stuff first.

Buy, hold and rent

If you are looking for cash flow, buy a bargain house as discussed above then rent it out. If you buy well in the right community, you will do very well. This category includes multi-units as well, but remember the rules are a bit different there. Check out **wrightthurston.com** if multi-units interest you. Before you pursue a buy-hold-rent strategy, take stock of your temperament and decide whether or not you would like to be a landlord. If you do it right and you are consistent and fair, it will be a good experience for you.

Foreclosures

This is a big money maker. It takes a lot of work and can be a cash intensive proposition, but it has some great upsides including very high profit. You have to be willing to deal with people in high stress situations, but the return can be well worth it. You can buy foreclosures three different ways: Pre-foreclosures, At the Auction and After the Auction. To learn the ethical and moral ways of doing this type of transaction – where you actually help people rather than harming them – check out Zick's materials. Of course, you need an "exit" strategy. Most people flip these properties, but some hold and rent them with very nice cash flow results.

Tax foreclosures

In 31 states, when properties are foreclosed by the county the property is sold off. This works much like the mortgage foreclosures mentioned above, but the auctions are less frequent and are conducted by the county in which the property resides.

Carrying paper

You can buy discounted mortgages and use the cash flow from these. I have looked into this, but I am not an expert. Nor have I ever done it. The return sounds really good, however, and I might pursue this strategy in the future. Check out Zick's materials to learn more about this strategy. This strategy requires you to have some ready cash and is probably better suited to folks who have the disposable cash available.

Tax Lien certificates

This is my favorite vehicle under the Real Estate category and we have had some fine success. In 19 states – as of this writing – rather than foreclosing on a property when a tax is not paid, the county will sell the lien to private investors. The interest rates are quite attractive. Our average rate this past year was 17-18 percent. Not bad. Rates can go up 50 percent or more! If you are interested in learning more, we are developing our own Tax Lien materials and you can contact us at **taxlien@anbeyond.com** and we will put you on our list until we have more information.

Obviously other strategies are available. I hope you can see why the Real Estate arena is so attractive. It is one of the few places where you can work deals immediately and make money without a large initial investment.

THE STOCK MARKET

A number of Stock Market strategies can provide good investment vehicles. My wife is doing quite well with this, but I don't touch it. You have to love numbers and you have to know how to research and research and research... get the picture? I will mention three strategies here that seem to be great ways to go. Keep in mind I am not endorsing these strategies. I just know people who have succeeded with them.

Dollar cost averaging

This is a long-term strategy designed to give you good returns over a long period. It takes usually a minimum of five to six years, but the returns increase as the years go by.

Simply put, Dollar Cost Averaging is the buying and holding of Stocks on a regular basis. Let's say you buy the same group of Stocks at a set dollar amount, regardless of the current price - over an extended period of time as mentioned above. You will come out ahead in nearly every case.

If you mirror the S&P 500 with this strategy, you have a good chance of outperforming the market in general. It has been shown that the S&P 500 over extended time will outperform the market.

To simplify it even further. Buy shares of indexed funds that are traded like Stocks – i.e., SPY and QQQ – and you will get the return you desire over the extended time.

A great way to follow this strategy is by using **www.sharebuilder.com**. You can invest any amount there. I have found this to be the best way of following the DCA strategy without getting involved in heavy broker fees. Just remember that you do need to get the education to do this and that this tiny description is not enough to constitute a reasonable strategy.

Dogs of the Dow

The website **www.dogsofthedow.com** describes this strategy well. Here is what they have to say on their website:

> Investing in the Dogs of the Dow is relatively simple. After the stock market closes on the last day of the year, of the 30 stocks that make up the Dow Jones Industrial Average, select the ten stocks which have the highest dividend yield. Then simply get in touch with your broker and invest an equal dollar

> amount in each of these ten high yield stocks. Then hold these ten 'Dogs of the Dow' for one year. Repeat these steps each and every year.
> – *Dog Steps* from
> www.dogsofthedow.com/dogsteps.htm

It is a very interesting strategy and quite simple. I know a few people who have followed this strategy. They have been happy even in the tough times of the last few years. Again, get an informed opinion before doing this. Study is the key.

Options Trading

This is probably the most "sexy" of the strategies discussed here. Simply put, you buy and/or sell the right to buy or sell a Stock at a certain price in a given amount of time. This is a speculative strategy. Most of the people I know who succeed with this strategy do it on an extremely short-term basis. Marita has been studying this strategy and will soon be doing some of it with part of our "high risk" fund. It has great potential for high return, but it is not without risk. Be careful here, but it is worth a look! Check out **www.onlineoption.com** for one system that seems to be effective.

FRANCHISES

I am not the biggest fan of franchises, but some might be good moneymakers. After all, many people have made very nice livings with gas stations and fast food franchises. Today you can find franchises for just about anything. If you feel that you need the help of a franchise, go for it. But be careful. Franchise fees and required advertising coops can be costly and add to large overhead expense. Do the research and if you find a franchise that looks promising, do your very best to negotiate down both fees. The ***Franchising for Dummies*** book looks very good. It is written by Dave Thomas of

Wendy's fame and his coauthor Michael Seid. Thomas has a well-earned reputation as a good guy in the franchise world, so his book would be my first stop if I were looking in that direction.

INTERNET

Ever since the dot.com boom of the 90's fizzled out, many people believe the Internet is not the place to make money. Don't tell that to the thousands of people doing it! The difference today is that successful entrepreneurs approach the Internet with better, more solid plans, rather than the wishful thinking that characterized the dot.com craze.

The Internet can make you money in so many ways that it's hard to suggest where to start. You can sell your own products online. You can sell products for others via franchises and affiliate programs. You choose where to begin.

Regardless of how you approach the Internet, you need to learn marketing. You will find many market resources out there, but I recommend starting with ***Low-Budget Online Marketing*** by Holly Berkley and ***Streetwise Low-Cost Web Site Promotion: Every Possible Way to Make Your Web Site a Success, Without Spending Lots of Money*** (Adams Streetwise Series) by Barry Feig. Both are good starting points for your research.

SELLING ONLINE WITHOUT A WEBSITE

There are two businesses are suited particularly to the Internet. They are important enough to give them their own discussion as separate income streams in the two sections that follow.

Selling things on eBay is cool because the concept is so simple. I often buy major items off eBay because of the price advantage, the convenience and the fun! Of course eBay is not the only player in town. Amazon.com and some of the other large sites out there provide an easy, low-cost way to sell stuff online.

Here are two books that can help you: ***Starting an eBay Business for Dummies*** by Marsha Collier and ***Selling Used Books Online: The Complete Guide to Bookselling at Amazon's Marketplace and Other Online Sites*** by Stephen Windwalker. You might also use this stream as a test for your future online business. It is a wonderful way to get into selling on the Internet with very little money or risk.

NETWORK MARKETING

To me, Network Marketing is an amazing fit for the Internet. While I am not involved in a Network Marketing program at this time, I know a number of people who are doing well in this arena. Via the internet, you can be very personal and it is an excellent tool for taking care of your down line. In my experience, the best resource is Daren Falter at **www.networkmarketingonthenet.com**. Daren is a good man and a veritable Network Marketing genius. If you are interested in this stream, his site is the place to start.

INVENTIONS

One of my heroes growing up was Thomas Edison. I always wanted to be an inventor but never quite made it. You just might have the million-dollar idea, however. If this is something that works for you, go for it, but be aware of the pitfalls. Cover your intellectual property with prudent care. Get your ideas patented and document everything.

****

A man is a success if he gets up in the morning and gets to bed at night, and in between he does what he wants to do.

– Bob Dylan

To get started, check out ***The Complete Idiot's Guide(R) to Cashing in On Your Inventions*** by Richard C. Levy. I took a good look through it a while back and it seems to cover all the basics. You might also check out ***The Inventor's Bible: How to Market and License Your Brilliant Ideas*** by Ronald Louis, Sr. Docie and J. W. Downs. I have been told this is a great resource. As with most of the books I have discussed on the previous pages, these are not endorsements, just a suggested starting place.

LICENSING

If you are not an inventor but you want to work with inventions and new ideas, why not learn how to license them for profit? A number of people do this profitably. I have not done much with this, but it appears to be a great way to use your imagination and to work with an inventor. The following book seems to be the best introductory text that came up in my search: ***How to License Your Million Dollar Idea: Everything You Need To Know To Turn a Simple Idea into a Million Dollar Payday***, 2nd edition by Harvey Reese.

CONSULTING

If you want financial independence but still like the field you have been working in full time, why not become a highly paid expert? Become a consultant and contract back into your company or do similar work for other companies. If you have the right skill set, you can go into companies and troubleshoot and advise rather than just being a worker bee. The possibilities are endless.

Best of all, you have flexibility. You can work part time or full time; onsite or off; long term or short. You can also work for yourself or through an agency. Your choices are numerous. The one thing you do need is a clear understanding of what you do and how to market it. Here are some books to help you get started: ***Getting Started in Consulting*** by Alan Weiss and ***The Consultant's Quick Start Guide: An Action Plan for Your First Year in Business*** by Elaine Biech.

MENTORING AND COACHING

At one time many types of work fell under the name "consulting." But in recent years, coaching and mentoring have taken on greater importance in the American business culture. While a consultant comes in to perform a function or advise on a specific action, a coach is brought in to facilitate in some capacity. Like a football coach, he doesn't play, but he makes a big difference in the game.

Depending on the type of coaching that interests you, it might be wise to get a certification. Different types of coaching certifications are available. Search the web on this subject and check out these books: ***Coaching and Mentoring for Dummies*** by Marty Brounstein, and ***Personal Coaching for Results: How to Mentor and Inspire Others to Amazing Growth*** by Louis E. Tice and Joyce Quick.

TRADE FAIRS AND FESTIVALS

I have a friend who runs sports shows and Christmas shows from Alaska to the Southwest and I am amazed at what he does. I am also amazed at how well the vendors do at his events. The more I hear from him, the more

****

Successful people do not waste time,
nor do they suffer those who waste time,
but they are compassionate and care deeply about those in need...
and a person who is truly in need,
by definition, is not wasting time.
- Roger Mallory

I find that these are great streams as well as excellent marketing opportunities. Do you have a craft that you are good at or do you have a unique product that you don't know how to market? Go to a craft fair or arts fair or some other type of festival and you will have gone a long way toward getting that product marketed. A good place to start with this stream is a periodical called *The Crafts Report* at www.craftsreport.com . I know of no good books on the subject, but I will keep an eye out for one!

A quick word about asset protection

Earlier in the book, I mentioned asset protection. While this is not an income stream, it is an important way to retain the money you earn. Learning how to incorporate and to use corporate structures in a legal and ethical way is an important aspect of your future work. Please take the time to research this. You will be surprised at how much you will save and how well you and your family will be protected financially.

A final word

I hope these last few pages have given you ideas for thought. I also hope you are excited, for you have much to be excited about. Things are changing in our business world today and I believe the small business entrepreneur is the future for many of us. Furthermore, I want to share the one truth that has been a breakthrough in my life over the last few years. The only person who sets limits for me is *me*. If you believe in yourself, you will accomplish great things. And you just might accomplish all your dreams along the way!

Take care, and much success to you!

Our Lessons from Our Six Weeks

By the time you read this, we will have completed the Six Week Adventure that has been the primary focus for Marita and me. I want to reflect on some of the lessons we learned. I also want to tell you what we are planning for this site in the coming weeks!

Lesson 1 – Wealth building is about attitude. Yes, we want to make money just like the next person. Of course we don't want to be destitute! I will say to you that when you are trying to build wealth and live prosperously – it is about attitude. The reason I say this is that a lot of people out there should be filthy rich right now. They are not because they choose not to see the possibilities. A prosperous person is one who sees how things can be done.

Lesson 2 – Don't quit! There is much competition out there and it is easy to get discouraged. If you believe in what you are doing and if you have a product that has value, you have a chance. However, most people give up way too easily. You will experience frustrations and lulls and disappointments. Don't let them deter you from your goals! This is one of those things I believe God has done for us. In the midst of the human condition we are taught through struggle to persevere. At the end is the reward. This is one of those lessons that spills over into every nook and cranny of our lives. Don't quit. Don't give in. Don't allow yourself to be discouraged. You will find that the reward is great and your blessings will reach beyond you to others.

Lesson 3 – Learn to prioritize. Listen to tapes. Read books. Then learn the 80/20 rule. For anyone out there who doesn't know what the 80/20 rule is, let me give it to you. 80% of the stuff that matters is accomplished by 20% of the work. Learn to do that 20% first. Now I know a number of you will say to me, "Roger, this is basic stuff." My reply is this: "If it is so basic, are you doing it?" MY wager is that most of you are not yet doing this. I am not. I am getting better, but it is a difficult thing to get used to. If every night you can identify 10 to 15 things that you "need" to do the next day, you are way ahead of most. If you can prioritize them, you are one of the few. If you can ID the 20%, you will be one of the world's most successful people.

Lesson 4 – Value your family and your time. This relates to

lesson 3. Be sure to include your family in what you are doing. Take the time to do non-work stuff. I do think those people who take Sundays off will be the most successful in the long run. I have gotten to know a number of Jewish people over the years and they are very insistent on observing the Sabbath. For that one day they honor God and their families. Learn to observe your own Sabbath day whether you are Christian, Jewish or whatever. Allow yourself this time and it will be returned to you in amazing ways.

Lesson 5 – Have a plan. Write your mission statements, business plans and marketing plans. We didn't pay enough attention to this but we are now. Create a main mission statement. Then do one for each business you have. Then do your business plans and marketing plans. They don't have to be big and they don't have to be fancy. They do have to be action and goal oriented. We are developing a one-page form for the business plan. There is a great one-page marketing plan in the ONE MININUTE MILLIONAIRE. If your business is simple, you can do everything in two pages. It is not that difficult to do. Allow yourself to make it simple, but do it. Then review it regularly and keep track of your growth. You will be amazed!

Lesson 6 – It is okay to shoot for the stars and it is also okay to come up short and only hit the moon. Big ideas become big realities if you dare to pursue them. Set your goals, then set a few of them bigger than you think you can make. Stretch a little bit and you will be surprised. And if you fail, remember that it is only failure if you learn nothing from it. Take what you learn, use it and you will win.

So, these are the six lessons we learned from our adventure. Now we are moving on to working the businesses we established during the six weeks. We should make our goal of $1, 000, 000 by the end of the summer. Thus, we will be documenting the coming months on a weekly basis. We will also be working on the book. We are excited with all the material we have accumulated. We also hope to get our special, limited edition e-book out in the coming weeks as well. In other words, we are not slowing down at all!

Take care and thank you for all of your wonderful support over the last six weeks!

P.S. There are many great and talented people out there and they don't have the desire to market their talents. What if you partnered with them? They create the product and you do the marketing and split the profits. This is similar to the licensing idea, except you join with them in the project rather than just licensing the product. In a way, just as a ghostwriter writes, you can be a ghostmarketer!

APPENDICES

Personally I'm always ready to learn,
although I do not always like being taught.
- Sir Winston Churchill

APPENDIX I – YOUR HOME OFFICE

To do any venture from your home, you will need to set up a home office. Here are some things to consider in setting up your workspace:

I. Check with the IRS as to what qualifies as a home office for tax purposes. Personally, we play it safe in our house by having a separate room dedicated as our home office. We keep all our business-related equipment in that room. We conduct business from that room 90% of the time. In other words, when we enter that room, we are going to work. If you can't do this, there are restrictions on what qualifies. Get the information from the IRS and your accountant and follow the rules. A good place to start is **www.irs.gov/newsroom/article/0, , id=108138, 00.html**.

II. Get a good computer. Most likely you have a computer, but is it good enough? Specifications are tricky, so I will not give those, but here are some capabilities you need to consider:

1. The screen must be big enough and clear enough. Clarity is more important. I come out of the computer industry and I now need reading glasses resulting from years of staring at bad monitors. If you can afford it, get an LCD monitor. It is even worth sacrificing size for the clarity. Your eyes are a valuable asset. Take care of them!

2. Does your computer have the speed and memory for your required applications? A good rule of thumb is to double the minimum processor, memory and disk requirements for the most demanding program you expect to use. If your program requires a minimum of a 333mHz processor, 256 meg of RAM and 1 meg of disk space, your computer should be at least 650mHz, 512meg of Ram and your hard drive should have at least 2 meg of free space for the program. Actually, I would hope your hard drive is not nearly that full!

3. Is your printer economical for business use? Ink-jet printers are great for color and pictures, but they are expensive for such things as letters and receipts! Go buy a cheap laser printer instead. They are available used or new in a number of places. I have seen several entry-level models in the $100 range. It will be worth it and you can keep your inkjet for producing pictures and color items that you will need in the future.

4. Is your Internet connection high-speed? In this day and age, your computer is a vital tool for

communications and purchasing. Spend the little extra for high speed DSL or Cable access. The time you save will pay for the difference.

5. Get a good bookkeeping package. Consult your accountant for this. There are other things to consider as well, but you can get plenty of advice from vendors and software suppliers. If you really feel that you can't trust the guy down at the local shop, feel free to drop me a note at rogermallory@anbeyond.com.

III. Get a fax machine. Actually, we have combined our fax needs into a multiuse machine that includes a laser printer and scanner. This kills two birds with one stone. We don't use it for receiving at this time, but we do send a lot through it.

IV. Get a separate business line if you plan to continue on the entrepreneurial path that we advocate in this book. Have it billed separately. It is easier as well. Further, use voicemail rather than a recorder and even better, get multiple voicemail boxes. These are invaluable for marketing or if you are doing more than one stream of income.

V. Get a good filing cabinet and some bookshelves. Record keeping is very important and an admitted weakness for us. Keep records of everything and take the time to keep learning.

VI. Get a great chair. Use any table if it is the right height and even your bookcases and file cabinets can be old and used, but get a chair that is comfortable for you. As I recommended for your computer monitor, do not compromise on this item! You will be using it a lot and you should be comfortable. A good chair that you will love can cost as little as $150. Even if it is $1, 000, get it as soon as you can. It will make a huge difference!

V. Lighting. Be sure your office is well lit. You should also have a window with some natural light thrown in if possible. Avoid florescent lighting if you can. Its cycling nature causes eyestrain similar to that caused by CRT computer monitors.

The above should get you started. Obviously you will have other considerations, but this is a good start. When you reach a sticking point, you might check a bookstore for some books on the subject as well as the numerous magazines on home-based businesses.

APPENDIX II – GOAL SETTING PRIMER

HERE IS A GOAL SETTING PROCESS YOU CAN USE.
You can also find this information
in Issues 12, 13 and 14 of our newsletter at
www.anbeyond.com/Newsletters/nlindex.htm

A quick goal setting primer

Probably one of the most important things I have learned is the power of setting goals. If you have ever heard Mark Victor Hansen speak, you know just how important he believes goal setting to be. The last time I heard him, he said he currently had over 2000 goals! Not only that, he was still adding to the list.

With only 75 goals, Marita and I are amateurs in comparison. Never fear, we will have more. It is an incredibly rich subject; so let me share with you the keys to successful goal setting I have used.

Write them down

The human memory is perplexing, complex and sometimes imprecise. Don't trust your memory as the only way to remember your goals. Learn to write them down. Use a spreadsheet, a word processor, a notebook or whatever vehicle you want. Just be sure to write them down in a place where you can read, modify and add to the list.

For illustration purposes, let's use a notebook as our model. Each page should have a minimum of three columns: One for the date you commit the goal to paper, one to describe your goal, and one that will allow you to record the date it is fulfilled. You can add other features to your list, of course. It is, after all, your notebook.

Do the dreaming first

Set aside your notebook for a while and get a pad of paper. You should do this exercise by yourself. If you are married, your spouse should do the same by his/herself. Do your best not to compartmentalize your goals. They can be professional, personal, relational, recreational, or anything else you can think of. Be visionary. Choose the impossible for some of them. Let them flow. After you finish, set your list aside for a day or two, then take it out again and tweak it.

Next, sit down with your spouse or a trusted friend or family member and review your goals. Remember, these are your goals and – with the exception of your spouse – the contributor you have chosen is simply there to help you expand the goals you have set down. They are not there to criticize. Your spouse has the privilege of veto but hopefully this will be constructive. Couples also need to merge their lists at some level. This is something you can negotiate with each other. My wife and I are very supportive of each other's goals and we view our lists as one.

Now you have a list you have reviewed and expanded. It is time for the next step.

Presort them

Take time to circle the goals you think are within reach. Don't get rid of the other goals that appear right now to be impossible. Just keep them on a list to be used later. Believe me, they are not impossible. At worst, they are simply improbable right now. Things will look different later.

Organize them

Now, pick up your notebook and label one page each with the following labels:

One Month
Three Months
Six Months
One Year
Two Years
Five Years
And Beyond

Take your dream list and add the circled items onto the appropriate pages. Do this with your spouse if you are married. I encourage you to handwrite this. That way, you will have written it twice. As you write them the second time, read them out loud. The more times and ways you interact with the material, the further into your mind the material will go and the better you will remember it.

If this is all you do, you will be light years ahead of so many other people. But don't stop here.

Look at the goals you have written. There sure are a lot of them, aren't there? When I first wrote down my goals, I became very much aware that a lot of pretty cool things were in store for me. I hope what you have done so far has inspired you, because the fun is just beginning!

Earlier, you took the less accessible goals and put them on a separate piece of paper. Grab that list and take a good look at it. After reading these goals again, write at the top of that list: ***The Possible Impossible List!*** Review these once a week in the coming months. You will find they seem much more reachable than they appeared when you first wrote them down. As they become more possible, take them from the list and add them to your regular lists. Feel free to update your lists at your leisure!

Now that you have seven or more pages of lists, take one list each night for the next week and prioritize them. Number them down the page. If you are doing this with your spouse, take the time to talk about the top three. Talk in pictures about them.

If you are alone, I want to encourage you to talk to a significant person about them. Of course, we all have private goals and it is good not to share those. But do share those that can be shared.

Envision

Now take some time to envision your goals. Draw a picture. Write a paragraph or two. Cut out pictures from a magazine and use a relevant photo as wallpaper on your computer. Do anything to help you to remember your goals. The more creative you are in this exercise, the better. If one of your five-year goals is a new house, describe what it looks like, where it is located, what color it is and how it is furnished. Make as complete a picture as you can.

Now take action

See those lists? Take the first goal on the first list, make a plan and go do it. Get started now. Don't wait! Create within yourself a sense of expectancy. Go for it! Enough cliché's for you yet? This message is absolutely vital! After you have your goals written out, you must go do them. Take them one at a time. Plan them. *But do the work.* You will not accomplish your goals by sitting and staring at them.

When you accomplish a goal

When you accomplish a goal, write it down next to the original goal. If you arc thc journaling sort, add your accomplishment to your journal. After a few months and on into the years, you will be able to look back at this list and draw strength and inspiration. You will laugh and you might also shed a tear. Regardless, you will find the experience rewarding.

Revisit and review

Revisit your list from time to time. The more often you do this the better. Weekly is quite a commitment, but if you can do it the rewards are great. Make it an enjoyable task. Sit yourself in front of the fire or on the front porch. Go through your list and keep it up to date.

Review your "in progress" goals daily. Memorize them but also keep them in front of you as much as you can. Put them on the refrigerator and on the bathroom mirror.

It is important to do two additional things

First, make all your goals measurable in some way. In the corporate culture, these measurements are called deliverables. Use that label if you like. I tend to think of them as identifiable outcomes. In other words, it is easy to figure the achievement of buying the first investment property. You bought the house, condo or other property. This does not work well with ideas such as spending more quality time with a spouse. Rather, I seek to gauge this by observing my wife. Is she happy? Does she get to do the things that she likes? If I can answer these questions, I know I am there!

It is a good idea to write down some of these measures along with your goals. It is helpful and encouraging.

Second, learn to celebrate! Throughout the world each culture has celebrations. Many religions have the right of passage for their children to adulthood. For a short time, I was the youth pastor for a Lutheran church in Arcadia, California. I can remember going from home to home on Confirmation Sunday. It was amazing – cars and thousands of dollars and all manner of gifts!

We celebrate holidays. We enjoy birthdays. We dedicate our children to God. Learn to celebrate the accomplishment of your goals as they happen. Go out to dinner, take a weekend trip, do something to commemorate the occasion. You will find that this will help you on your way to achieving more goals. You might also discover that you are motivated to work much harder towards those goals!

Happy Goal Setting!

APPENDIX III – CREATIVE GIVING IDEAS

What follows is a list of 27 different ways you can give back to your community, an act that will result in abundance and good fortune for you. This list just scratches the surface. I expect you can come up with ten other ideas for each one below!

****

Reduce your plan to writing...
The moment you complete this,
you will have definitely given concrete form
to the intangible desire.
- Napoleon Hill

11 WAYS TO GIVE ON A DAILY BASIS

1. **Say Hello to someone and use his /her name if you can**
2. **Smile**
3. **Compliment someone**
4. **Hold back a criticism – just don't say it**
5. **Buy someone a cup or coffee, juice or a soft drink**
6. **Do as favor cheerfully when asked**
7. **Buy a promotional item such as a candy bar to support a child's interest in Little League or scouting**
8. **Buy lunch for a homeless person**
9. **Say "please" and "thank you"**
10. **Say "Have a nice day" to the checkout clerk and use his/her name if you can**
11. **Open the door for someone**

Write in some of your own:

____

____

____

____

____

____

____

____

9 LARGER WAYS YOU CAN GIVE

1. Visit an elderly person
2. Help serve dinner at a shelter
3. Buy a poor kid a bike
4. Volunteer you talents to a local project – carpenters doing repairs at the local YMCA for example
5. Give a jobless person a lift to an interview
6. Buy dinner for the local shelter coordinator
7. Baby sit for a young couple so they can have a night out
8. Place flowers at veterans' gravesites
9. Organize and host a neighborhood barbeque

Write in some of your own:

7 REGULAR WAYS YOU CAN GIVE

1. **Tithe – Give 10% of your earnings to your church or favorite charity**
2. **Head and/or participate in a committee for your church or favorite charity**
3. **Take an elderly person out to lunch on a regular basis**
4. **Offer your talents and skills on a regular on-call basis to a needy organization**
5. **Take a regular shift at the local food bank**
6. **Offer to counsel others on job and trade skills at a shelter or other organization**
7. **Repair cars for residents of a women's shelter**

Write in some of your own:

____

____

____

____

____

____

I know you will find something here that you will do or will be a catalyst for you to make a real difference in your community. Do remember one thing: Even a smile given in kindness is a golden gift that is utterly unique to you and is yours to give freely. Make the world a better place to live and you will live a better life!

APPENDIX IV – RESOURCES

What follows on these pages is a list of a number of resources that were of great help to the writing of this book and the efforts behind the Six Week Adventure. I hope that they will be of use to you as well.

BOOKS:

Think and Grow Rich **by Napoleon Hill**
Mass Market Paperback: 256 pages
Publisher: Fawcett Books; Reissue edition (November 1990); ISBN: 0449214923

If there is one book besides ours that can help you plan for your Adventure, this is the one. Very few people understand it after the first reading. After you read through it a few times, you will be amazed how much you will learn.

Thou Shall Prosper:
Ten Commandments for Making Money **by Rabbi Daniel Lapin; Hardcover: 362 pages**
Publisher: John Wiley & Sons
1st edition (September 13, 2002); ISBN: 0471218685

A Jewish Rabbi takes the reader through the traditional Jewish view of money. This is a great book to help understand how to deal with the destructive myths about money in modern society.

Create Your Own Future: How to Master the 12 Critical Factors of Unlimited Success
by Brian Tracy; Hardcover: 288 pages
Publisher: John Wiley & Sons
1st edition (August 16, 2002); ISBN: 0471251070

This is a must read primer on success. It is well written and a quick read.

The Psychology of Persuasion:
How to Persuade Others to Your Way of Thinking
by Kevin Hogan; Hardcover: 280 pages
Publisher: Pelican Pub Co; (June 1996)
ISBN: 1565541464

This is the best book out there for learning the techniques of persuasion. Hogan is a wonderful writer. This book is also the easiest to read and understand. While Cialdini's book – recommended below – is more in depth than this one, it is also more academic and more difficult to wade through. We suggest you listen to the audio version. It is very well done and will allow you to hear the inflection of various phrases.

Failing Forward: How to Make the Most of Your Mistakes
by John C. Maxwell
Hardcover: 209 pages; Publisher: Thomas Nelson
(March 8, 2000); ISBN: 0785274308

The Power of Focus
by Jack Canfield, Les Hewitt, Mark Victor Hansen
Paperback: 310 pages
Publisher: Health Communications; (April 2000);
ISBN: 1558747524

Getting Everything You Can Out of All You've Got: 21 Ways You Can Out-Think, Out-Perform, and Out-Earn the Competition
by Jay Abraham
Hardcover: 376 pages; Publisher: St. Martin's Press (February 2000); ISBN: 0312204655

Influence (rev): The Psychology of Persuasion
by Robert B. Cialdini Phd (Author)
Paperback: 336 pages ;Publisher: Quill
Revised edition (September 1998); ISBN: 0688128165

Goals: How to Get Everything You Want — Faster Than You Ever Thought Possible
by Brian Tracy
Hardcover: 289 pages Publisher: Berrett-Koehler Pub
1st edition (March 2003); ISBN: 1576752356

AUDIO COURSE TAPES
from the masters. Check out eBay for some great prices on these. Normally very expensive, they are deeply discounted on eBay. Here are some examples:

Robert Allen	**Zig Zigler**	**Mark Victor Hansen**
Andrew Carnegie	**Jim Rohn**	**Ron LeGrand**
Jay Abraham	**Dan Kennedy**	**Stephen Covey**
Napoleon Hil	**Tom Hopkins**	**Earl Nightengale**
Denis Waitley	**Anthony Robins**	

WEBSITES

www.briantracy.com/ – His free audio CDs are awesome and worth getting. He also has some great newsletters.

multiplestreamsofincome.com – This is a great place to order the ***One Minute Millionaire*** book. The newsletter is so-so, but still interesting.

www.johnchilders.com – The free Real Estate course is an incredible deal for people interested in Real Estate investing. This is the real deal and you will find nothing better. Unfortunately, John is retired from the Real Estate seminar business, so the student will have to seek advanced information elsewhere.

www.ebay.com is a wonderful place to find tapes and materials for research. A quick search on just about any major author's name will get results. For example:

www.sba.gov – Website for the small business association.

www.mentorsmagazine.com – Great for inspiration.

www.score.org – Retired business people who help new entrepreneurs get their start.

www.networkmarketingonthenet.com – The best place to learn about Network Marketing that exists on the Internet. Some great classes.

www.techtamers.com – Some great stuff on Internet marketing. The free resources at **www.techtamers.com/free resources/index.htm** are worth the time if the Internet is of interest to you. Great newsletter.

www.tomantion.com – A great free course on Internet marketing.

www.markvictorhansen.com – A fantastic newsletter on success.

www.jimrohn.com – Another worthwhile newsletter!

BIBLIOGRAPHY

Awaken the American Dream
by Charles V. Douglas
Publisher: Markowski Intl; (September 2003)
ISBN: 0938716395 **Paperback:** 182 pages

Business Writing For Dummies®
by Sheryl Lindsell-Roberts
Publisher: For Dummies; (March 1999)
ISBN: 0764551345 **Paperback:** 360 pages

Cashflow Quadrant: Rich Dad's Guide to Financial Freedom
by Robert T. Kiyosaki, Sharon L. Lechter
Publisher: Warner Books; (April 1, 2000)
ISBN: 0446677477 **Paperback:** 251 pages

Coaching and Mentoring for Dummies
by Marty Brounstein
Publisher: For Dummies; 1st edition (May 15, 2000)
ISBN: 0764552236 **Paperback:** 328 pages

Conversations with Millionaires: What Millionaires Do to Get Rich, That You Never Learned About in School!
by Mike Litman, Jason Oman, Robert Allen
Publisher: Cwm Publishing; (October 30, 2001)
ISBN: 1931866007 **Paperback:** 238 pages

Create Your Own Future: How to Master the 12 Critical Factors of Unlimited Success
by Brian Tracy
Publisher: John Wiley & Sons; 1 edition (August 16, 2002)
ISBN: 0471251070 **Hardcover:** 288 pages

Creating Wealth
by Robert Allen
Publisher: Fireside; Revised and Updated edition (April 1986)
ISBN: 0671621009 **Paperback:** 304 pages

Die Broke : A Radical Four-Part Financial Plan
by Stephen Pollan, Mark Levine
Publisher: HarperBusiness; (November 1998)
ISBN: 0887309429 **Paperback:** 320 pages

Differentiate or Die : Survival in Our Era of Killer Competition
by Jack Trout
Publisher: John Wiley & Sons; 1 edition (March 17, 2000)
ISBN: 0471357642 **Hardcover:** 230 pages

Failing Forward: How to Make the Most of Your Mistakes
by John C. Maxwell
Publisher: Thomas Nelson; (March 8, 2000)
ISBN: 0785274308 **Hardcover:** 209 pages

Franchising For Dummies®
by Michael Seid, Dave Thomas
Publisher: For Dummies; (July 2000)
ISBN: 0764551604 **Paperback:** 378 pages

Getting Everything You Can Out of All You've Got: 21 Ways You Can Out-Think, Out-Perform, and Out-Earn the Competition
by Jay Abraham
Publisher: Griffin Trade Paperback; (October 2001)
ISBN: 0312284543 **Paperback:** 384 pages

Getting Started in Consulting
by Alan Weiss
Publisher: John Wiley & Sons; 1st edition (January 15, 2000)
ISBN: 0471384550 **Paperback:** 272 pages

Goals: How to Get Everything You Want — Faster Than You Ever Thought Possible
by Brian Tracy
Hardcover: 289 pages
Publisher: Berrett-Koehler Pub; 1st edition (March 2003)
ISBN: 1576752356

Guerrilla Publicity: Hundreds of Sure-Fire Tactics to Get Maximum Sales for Minimum Dollars
by Jay Conrad Levinson, Rick Frishman, Jill Lublin
Publisher: Adams Media Corporation; (June 2002)
ISBN: 1580626823 **Paperback:** 304 pages

Guerrilla Marketing for Writers : 100 Weapons to Help You Sell Your Work
by Jay Conrad Levinson, Rick Frishman, Michael Larsen
Publisher: Writers Digest Books; (October 2000)
ISBN: 089879983X **Paperback:** 224 pages

Guerrilla Marketing: Secrets for Making Big Profits from Your Small Business
by Jay Conrad Levinson
Publisher: Mariner Books; 3rd edition (October 21, 1998)
ISBN: 0395906253 **Paperback:** 400 pages

How to License Your Million Dollar Idea: Everything You Need To Know To Turn a Simple Idea into a Million Dollar Payday, 2nd Edition
by Harvey Reese
Publisher: John Wiley & Sons; 2nd edition (June 28, 2002)
ISBN: 0471204013 **Paperback:** 240 pages

How To Make Money In Stocks: A Winning System in Good Times or Bad, 3rd Edition
by William J. O'Neil
Publisher: McGraw-Hill Trade; 3rd edition (May 23, 2002)
ISBN: 0071373616 **Paperback:** 272 pages

How To Win Friends And Influence People
by Dale Carnegie
Publisher: Pocket Books; Reissue edition (May 1990)
ISBN: 0671723650

Inc. & Grow Rich!
by C. W. Allen (Editor), Cheri S. Hill, Diane Kennedy, Garett Sutton, Garrett Sutton, Allen. C.W., Diane Kennedy CPA, Garett Sutton Esq.
Publisher: Sage International
3rd edition (September 30, 1999)
ISBN: 0967187109 **Paperback:** 240 pages

Influence: Science and Practice (4th Edition)
by Robert B. Cialdini
Publisher: Pearson Allyn & Bacon; 4th edition (June 29, 2000)
ISBN: 0321011473 **Paperback:** 262 pages
Influence (rev) : The Psychology of Persuasion
by Robert B. Cialdini (Author)
Publisher: Quill; Revised edition (October 1998)
ISBN: 0688128165 **Paperback:** 336 pages

Inner Security and Infinite Wealth: Merging Self Worth and Net Worth
by Stuart Zimmerman, Jared Rosen
Publisher: SelectBooks; (September 2003)
ISBN: 1590790553

Investing in Real Estate, Fourth Edition
by Andrew McLean, Gary W. Eldred
Publisher: John Wiley & Sons; 4th edition (March 2003)
ISBN: 047132339X **Paperback:** 320 pages

Investing Online for Dummies, 4th Edition
by Kathleen Sindell
Publisher: For Dummies; 4th edition (July 2002)
ISBN: 0764516566 **Paperback:** 408 pages

LEARNED OPTIMISM : HOW TO CHANGE YOUR MIND AND YOUR LIFE
by Martin Seligman
Publisher: Free Press; Reissue edition (March 1, 1998)
ISBN: 0671019112 **Paperback:** 336 pages

Live Your Dreams
by Les Brown
Publisher: Avon; Reissue edition (February 1996)
ISBN: 0380723743 **Paperback:** 272 pages

Live Rich : Everything You Need to Know To Be Your Own Boss
by Stephen Pollan, Mark Levine
Publisher: HarperBusiness; (January 2000)
ISBN: 0887309348 **Paperback:** 320 pages

Low-Budget Online Marketing
by Holly Berkle
Publisher: Self Counsel Press; (May 1, 2003)
ISBN: 1551804271 **Paperback:** 127 pages

Magic Of Thinking Big
by David Schwartz
Publisher: Fireside; Reprint edition (May 1987)
ISBN: 0671646788 **Paperback:** 192 pages ;
Multiple Streams of Income: How to Generate a Lifetime of Unlimited Wealth
by Robert G. Allen
Publisher: John Wiley & Sons; 1st edition (March 15, 2002)
ISBN: 0471218871 **Paperback:** 352 pages

Multiple Streams of Internet Income
by Robert G. Allen
Publisher: John Wiley & Sons; 1 edition (April 5, 2002)
ISBN: 0471410144 **Paperback:** 288 pages

Nothing Down 90s
by Robert Allen
Publisher: Simon & Schuster; Revised edition (November 1990)
ISBN: 0671725580 **Hardcover:** 368 pages

Own Your Own Corporation: Why the Rich Own Their Own Companies and Everyone Else Works for Them
by Garrett Sutton, Ann Blackman, Robert T. Kiyosaki
Publisher: Warner Books; (October 2001)
ISBN: 0446678619 **Paperback:** 352 pages

Permission Marketing : Turning Strangers Into Friends And Friends Into Customers
by Seth Godin
Publisher: Simon & Schuster; 1 edition (May 6, 1999)
ISBN: 0684856360 **Hardcover:** 256 pages

Personal Coaching for Results: How to Mentor and Inspire Others to Amazing Growth
by Louis E. Tice, Joyce Quick, Lou Tice
Publisher: Thomas Nelson; (January 1997)
ISBN: 0785273557 **Hardcover:** 320 pages

PSYCHO CYBERNETICS
by Maxwell Maltz
Publisher: Pocket Books; Reissue edition (August 1989)
ISBN: 0671700758

Rich Dad's Guide to Investing: What the Rich Invest in, That the Poor and the Middle Class Do Not!
by Robert T. Kiyosaki, Sharon L. Lechter
Publisher: Warner Books; (June 2000)
ISBN: 0446677469 **Paperback:** 384 pages

Rich Dad's Prophecy: Why the Biggest Stock Market Crash in History Is Still Coming... and How You Can Prepare Yourself and Profit from It!
by Robert T. Kiyosaki, Sharon L. Lechter
Publisher: Warner Books; (October 9, 2002)
ISBN: 0446530867 **Hardcover:** 304 pages

Retire Young, Retire Rich
by Robert T. Kiyosaki, Sharon L. Lechter
Publisher: Warner Books; 1st edition (January 15, 2002)
SBN: 0446678430 **Paperback:** 264 pages

Secrets of the Young & Successful : How to Get Everything You Want Without Waiting a Lifetime
by Jennifer Kushell, Scott Kaufman
Publisher: Fireside; (June 2003)
ISBN: 0743227581 **Paperback:** 368 pages

Selling Used Books Online: The Complete Guide to Bookselling at Amazon's Marketplace and Other Online Sites
by Stephen Windwalker
Publisher: Harvard Perspectives Press; (June 5, 2002)
ISBN: 0971577838 **Paperback:** 176 pages

Small Business for Dummies, 2nd edition
by Eric Tyson and Jim Schell
Publisher: For Dummies; 2nd edition (January 2, 2003)
ISBN: 0764554816 **Paperback:** 432 pages

Small Business Kit For Dummies®
by Richard D. Harroch
Publisher: For Dummies; Book and CD edition (Nov. 1998)
ISBN: 0764550934 **Paperback:** 400 pages

Starting an eBay Business for Dummies
by Marsha Collier (Author)
Publisher: For Dummies; 1st edition (Dec. 15, 2001)
ISBN: 0764515470 **Paperback:** 384 pages

Street-Smart Ethics: Succeeding in Business Without Selling Your Soul
by Clinton W. McLemore
Publisher: Westminster John Knox Press; 1st edition (Febr 2003) **ISBN:** 0664226280 **Paperback:** 186 pages

Streetwise Low-Cost Web Site Promotion: Every Possible Way to Make Your Web Site a Success, Without Spending Lots of Money (Adams Streetwise Series)
by Barry Feig
Publisher: Adams Media Corporation; (June 2001)
ISBN: 1580625010 **Paperback:** 368 pages

The Complete Idiot's Guide(R) to Cashing in On Your Inventions
by Richard C. Levy
Publisher: Alpha Communications; 1st edition (September 28, 2001)
ISBN: 0028642201 **Paperback:** 360 pages

The Complete Idiot's Guide to Managing Your Money (3rd Edition)
by Christy Heady, Robert K. Heady, Jody P. Schaeffer (Illustrator)
Publisher: Alpha Communications; 3rd edition (January 15, 2002)
ISBN: 0028642457 **Paperback:** 360 pages

The Complete Idiot's Guide to Real Estate Investing
by Stuart Leland Rider, Richard Mize, Chris Eliopoulos (Illustrator)
Publisher: Alpha Books; 2nd edition (May 6, 2003)
ISBN: 1592570631 **Paperback:** 380 pages

The Consultant's Quick Start Guide: An Action Plan for Your First Year in Business
by Elaine Biech
Publisher: Jossey-Bass/Pfeiffer; 1 edition (May 9, 2001)
ISBN: 0787956678 **Paperback:** 272 pages

The Inventor's Bible: How to Market and License Your Brilliant Ideas
by Ronald Louis, Sr. Docie, J. W. Downs
Publisher: Ten Speed Press; (August 2001)
ISBN: 1580083048 **Paperback:** 288 pages

The Laws of Money, The Lessons of Life: Keep What You Have and Create What You Deserve
by Suze Orman
Publisher: Free Press; (February 25, 2003)
ISBN: 0743245172 **Hardcover:** 336 pages

The Millionaire Course: A Visionary Plan for Creating the Life of Your Dreams
by Marc Allen, Mark Allen
Publisher: New World Library; (April 2003)
ISBN: 1577312325 **Paperback:** 320 pages

The Millionaire Mentor
by Greg S. Reid
Publisher: Markowski Intl; (September 2003)
ISBN: 0938716492 **Paperback:** 110 pages

The One Minute Millionaire: The Enlightened Way to Wealth
by Mark Victor Hansen, Robert G. Allen
Publisher: Harmony Books; 1st edition (Oct. 22, 2002)
ISBN: 0609609491 **Hardcover:** 416 pages

The Power of Focus
by Jack Canfield, Les Hewitt, Mark Victor Hansen
Publisher: Health Communications; (April 2000)
ISBN: 1558747524 **Paperback:** 310 pages

The Power of Your Subconscious Mind: One of the Most Powerful Self-Help Guides Ever Written!
by Joseph Murphy
Publisher: Bantam Books; Revised edition (Jan. 2, 2001)
ISBN: 0553583182 **Paperback:** 304 pages

The Psychology of Persuasion: How to Persuade Others to Your Way of Thinking
by Kevin Hogan
Publisher: Pelican Pub Co; (January 2003)
ISBN: 1565541464 **Hardcover:** 288 pages

The Warren Buffett Way : Investment Strategies of the World's Greatest Investor
by Robert G. Hagstrom
Publisher: John Wiley & Sons; Reprint edition (March 1997)
ISBN: 0471177504 **Paperback:** 274 pages

Think and Grow Rich
by Napoleon Hill
Publisher: Fawcett Books; Reissue edition (November 1990)
ISBN: 0449214923 **Paperback:** 256 pages

Thou Shall Prosper: Ten Commandments for Making Money
by Rabbi Daniel Lapin
Publisher: John Wiley & Sons; 1 edition (September 13, 2002)
ISBN: 0471218685 **Hardcover:** 362 pages

Unlimited Power : The New Science Of Personal Achievement
by Anthony Robbins
Publisher: Free Press; Reprint edition (December 22, 1997)
ISBN: 0684845776 **Paperback:** 448 pages

Walking with the Wise
by Linda Forsythe
Publisher: MENTORS Publications, Inc.; (May 23, 2003)
ISBN: 0972987509 **Paperback:** 320 pages

END NOTES

[1]Elizabeth Kubler-Ross, "Denial & Isolation Phase of Grief" 2002. About.com. http://dying.about.com/library/weekly/aa072897.htm

[2] Brian Tracy is one of the nation's foremost authorities on personal success and author of *Create Your Own Future* and *Victory!: Applying the Proven Principles of Military Strategy to Achieve Greater Success in Your Business and Personal Life.* These books can be purchased at http://www.anbeyond.com/BStore/B-index.htm.

[3] From *Resiliency: How To Bounce Back Faster, Stronger, Smarter,* by Tessa Albert Warschaw and Dee Barlow.

If you think you know the answers,
where's the motivation to learn?
- Conrad Schlumberger

Index

D

E

F

G

H

I

J

K

L

M

W

Y

Special Offer

for readers of this book

I am so convinced that you will want to make your new ventures work that we have developed a series of calls that we are calling the ***Takeoff to Your Future*** calls. These are one hour calls offered weekly to help you get started. Each call will address a single concept or source of income. All you have to do is log on to **www.anbeyond.com/callinfo** and you will be given instructions on how to participate in the calls. Here are the titles of some of the calls:

1. Wrassling the gator, help with getting over the doubts

2. Where to start with Real Estate

3. How to sell your house without using a Real Estate Agent

4. 10 people who must be a part of your team

5. Why Stocks are so important

6. Using Ebay to give you a fighting financial chance

7. Things that can go wrong

These are just a few of the calls we will be doing. We what this book to be one of the best experiences that you have ever had for learning to become a successful entreprenuer! These calls are yours for as long as you want as a way of us saying thank you for buying the book.

www.anbeyond.com/callinfo

Easy Order Form

Telephone Orders: 425-483-9943

Email Orders: Orders@AnBeyond.com

Mail Orders to: AnBeyond Publishing / attn: Orders
PMB 1227, 22833 Bothell Everett
Highway #102, Bothell, WA 98021

Please send the products at your current Prices:

____

____

____

____

Please send more FREE information on:

[ ] Other Books [ ] Speaking [ ] Mailing List [ ] Coaching

Name: ____

Address: ______________________________________

City: ____________________ State: ____ Zip: __________

Telephone: __________________________________

Email: _____________________________________

Sales Tax: Please add 8.8% for products shipped to Washington State addreses.

Shipping: Within US is $4.95 for first item and $2.95 for each additional item. Free shipping if order exceeds $200.00. International orders start at $12.95 and up depending on content of the order.

Payment: [ ] Visa [ ] Mastercard [ ] Check(include with order)

Card Number: ____________________________________

Name on Card: ___________________________________

Exp. Date: __________ Credit Card 3 Digit Check no.: ______

Without the help of the people on this page, this book would not have been impossible. I hope you may find a project to use them as well!

Cartoon Art,
Graphic Facilitation,
System, Concept and
Process Visualization

Michael Erickson
Visual Practitioner
Michael_Erickson.tripod.com

CrickettWorks
CREATIVE WRITING and EDITING GHOSTWRITING and PUBLISHING

Crickett E's	**Crickett Books**	**Crickett Biz**
Motivational e-books	Life stories and more	Creative marketing

Creative writing that opens doors... see where it takes you.

Launch your home business with an e-book * Take a creative approach to your marketing material * Turn your life story into a book * Brand yourself an expert with articles that tell a story * Sell your own book at your next speaking engagement

Let us custom-write or ghostwrite your next project:

E-Products to launch your business and change your life * Iternatives to traditional marketing materials * Books that help you promote your business and expertise * Compelling life stories * Mystery/suspense novels set at your company

We'll also edit your existing marketing materials or book manuscripts.

Let us know how we can help you!

Janet Helin
Writer, Editor, Ghostwriter
Independent Publisher
www.jwrites.com

Without this team of people, Russ the cover designer, Gene the logo designer and Russel of The Portrait, this book would be a great deal more boring!

Russ Warrick
Graphic Art & Design

Russ Warrick Graphic Art & Design specializes in all forms of print graphics. If you need corporate packages including business cards, logos, letterhead and envelopes, he can do it. He also has done book covers, product packaging, brochures as well as grand scale advertising for billboards and sporting. He can help you design your catalogs, price lists, CD cover art and calendars to name a few more.

Russ has been in the graphic design business for over 13 years. He specializes in taking time with those who know little or nothing. He can explain the process involved in taking your project from concept to the final printed piece. For information email him at russw@deepfrost.com.

DESIGN DESIGN

print

exhibit

web

425.827.0262
endicotz@gte.net
11324 NE 50th Pl.
Kirkland WA 98033
USA
Planet Earth

we bring ideas to life

http://mysite.verizon.net/res1dyjy/index.html

The Portrait

17630 140th Ave. NE Suite A
Woodinville, WA 98072
info@theportrait.net

(425) 481-9215